CAPE COD'S SECRET SPACES & MYSTERIOUS PLACES

A Guide to Little Known Historical,

Interesting and Sometimes Quirky Sites

and Places You Should Visit

Don E. Descy, Ph.D.

Bay View Editions
Travel Series
Fennbrook Media Group (USA), Ltd.
3 5 7 9 10 8 6 4 2

Printed in the United States of America
Editor: Adria Carey Perez, Odyssa, Orlando
Cover and Interior Design: Rafael Andres, CoverKitchen

While the author has made every effort to provide accurate and factual information this cannot be guaranteed.
ISBN (Paperback): 978-0-9994829-2-6
ISBN (eBook): 978-0-9994829-3-3

To my wife, Glenna,
Who has been with me all the way.

CONTENTS

INDEX

Sites By Content

Ghosts and Ghouls and Mysterious Shapes:

Historic Sites:

Legends and Lore

UPPER CAPE: BOURNE TO DENNIS

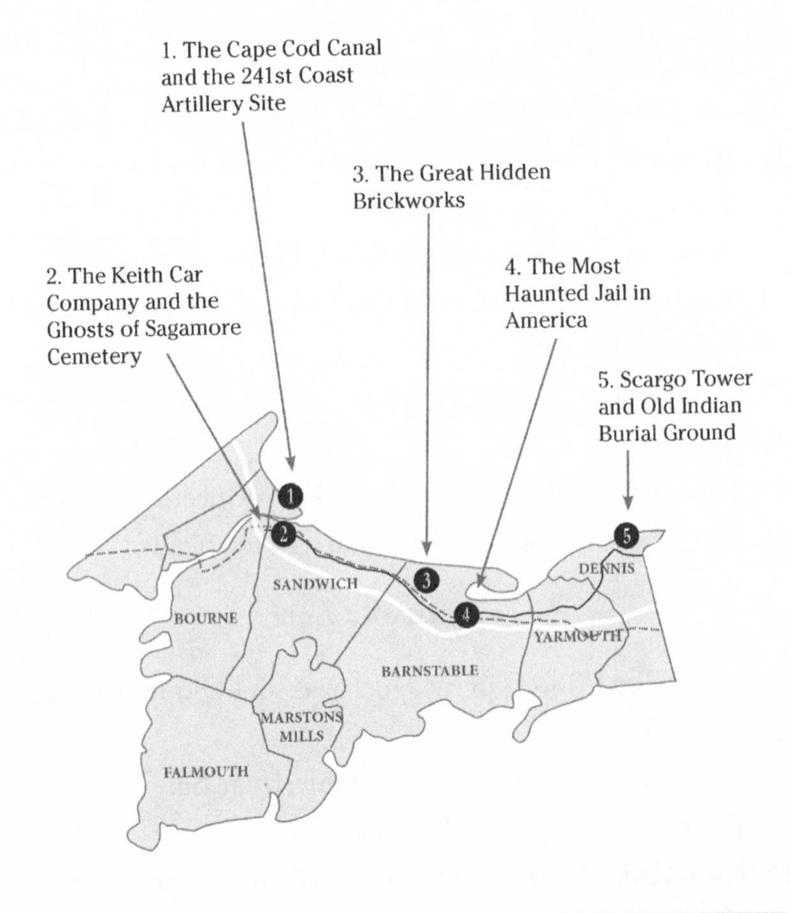

MID CAPE: BREWSTER TO WELLFLEET

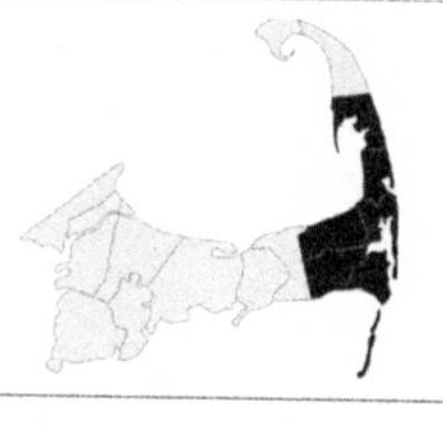

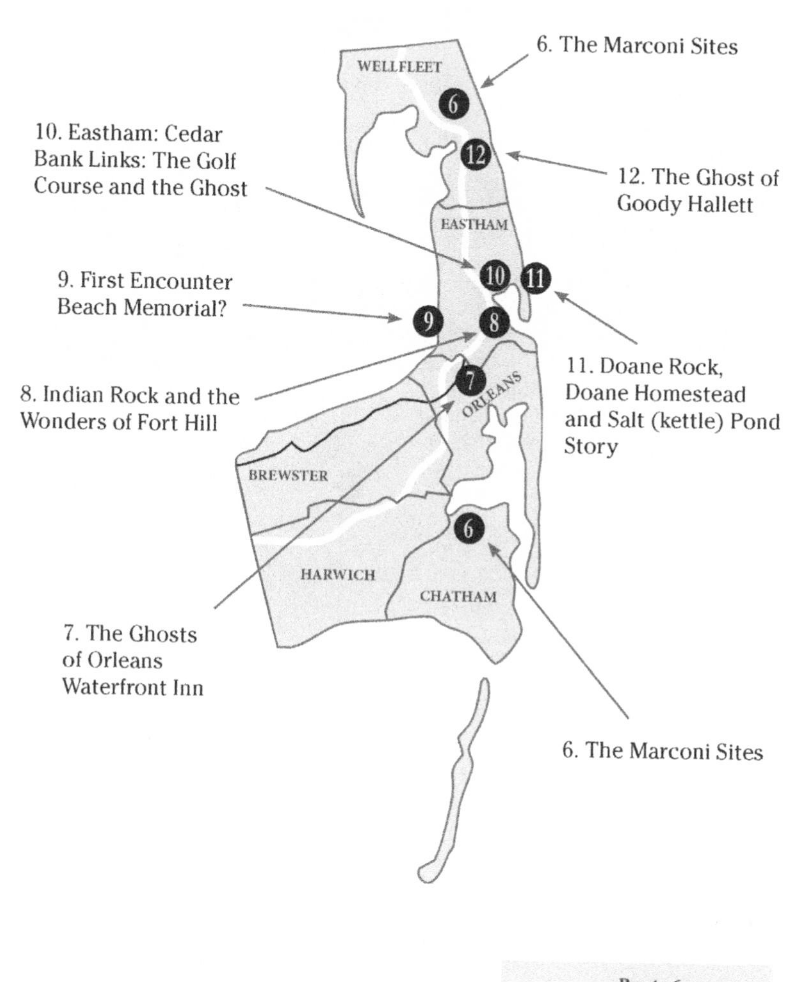

OUTER CAPE: TRURO AND PROVINCETOWN

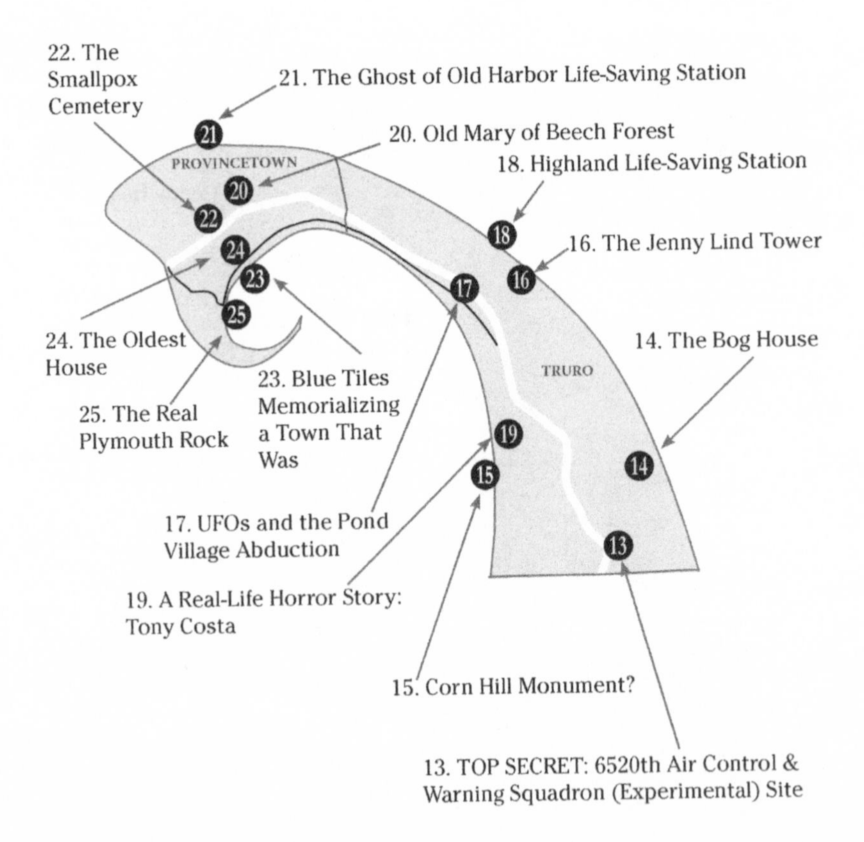

ACKNOWLEDGEMENTS

I wish to thank my editor, Adria Carey Perez, from Orlando, Florida for keeping me on the straight and narrow, and my Cover and Interior Designer, Rafael Andres from Mesa, Arizona, for putting up with all of my shortcomings. In addition, I want to thank my wife, Glenna, for final editing of the text and editing some of my photographs. I could not have done this without their help. The maps were the product of Andrea Pluhar of Wellfleet, Massachusetts, a truly Renaissance woman. She took my scribblings, turned them on their head, and gave me exactly what I wanted and the book needed.

I also wish to thank the Barnstable Historical Society, the Dennis Historical Society and the Eastham Historical Society for the images from their collections.

Thank you all!

FOREWORD

I love Cape Cod. You can come across the most unexpected things in the most unexpected places. Go off the beaten path, in many cases not very far, and you may be surprised what you might find: a strange collection of trinkets and coins at the base of a tree (gifts to a Wampanoag Princess), a graffiti covered wall in the middle of nowhere (a long forgotten major industrial site), a serene forest path near a quiet pond (an award-winning poet's inspirational place), metal roofed tunnels in the side of a hill (a World War II gun emplacement), orlittle blue tiles on the front of a house (houses that were floated across the harbor). Something of historical importance? Perhaps! Who knows?? Don't be surprised if you come across a small cemetery or a lone gravestone in the middle of nowhere–or just off the path. That granite post with the number ten on it? You will have to read on to find out about that one!

You may also see a historical monument that isn't. "This monument is where the first encounter between the Pilgrims and Native Americans took place." No, I will tell you and show you how to get to the real monument. "This monument is near the place where the starving Pilgrims took some corn so they could survive the winter." No, I will direct you to that real one, too. We will even talk about and locate a few ghosts, alien abductions, and

UFO encounter sites. Unexpected things in the most unexpected places...

I have had a good time finding these places, and I am sure that you will, too. I start our adventure at the Sagamore Bridge and end way out at the tip of the Cape; there are maps of all the locations at the beginning of this book. It is fun exploring new and different places. I picked twenty-five that I think you will find interesting. A few of them will even appear in hiking or walking guides.

But this book is not just a walking or hiking guide.

It is more like a travelogue through time. I have added history, stories, legends, and facts to help you understand the historical context of what you are reading and why I included them here. You may read something and say, "I just read that...". It is not in your head and not a mistake. Since some people may only read certain parts or parts out of order, I may have included the information that they may have missed in an earlier section.

Enjoy your travels, and if you have any questions, comments, or ideas for future places to explore, tweet me @don_descy.

A WORD ABOUT DATES

The Pilgrims arrived in Provincetown harbor on November 21 (O.S. November 11), 1620.

What in the world does "O.S." mean and why two different dates? O.S. is the abbreviation for the "Old Style" (Julian) calendar, just as N.S. is the abbreviation for the "New Style" (Gregorian) calendar. The Julian calendar was introduced by Julius Caesar in 46 BCE. The Gregorian calendar was introduced by Pope Gregory XII in 1582. In English historical research both calendar dates are usually shown. Nowadays, the most common method of dating around the world is the Gregorian (N.S.) calendar, which was first introduced into most English cultures in 1752.

Some interesting side notes:

In the British Empire, January 1 was not the first day of the year. It was March 25, that is until the 1752 calendar change! Before 1752, it was not uncommon for many people in England to celebrate the new year on January 1. That is why sometimes you might even see dates between January 1 and March 24 as the date and 1667/68 for the year (March 17, 1667/68, for example).

The Gregorian (N.S.) calendar was not adopted worldwide. The Julian (O.S.) calendar was traditionally used in Europe and its colonies. So...during the changeover from O.S. to N.S., and even today, many historians use both O.S and N.S. dates when they referred to historical events happening during that time.

Russia did not change its calendar from Julian (O.S.) to Gregorian (N.S.) until 1918, and many Eastern Orthodox churches still use the O.S. calendar even though the countries they are located in adopted the N.S. calendar in 1923. Greece was the last country to change over to the Gregorian (N.S.) calendar.

In 1620 the calendars differed by 10 days. Now they differ by 13 days.

1. SANDWICH: THE CAPE COD CANAL AND THE 241ST COAST ARTILLERY SITE

Historic Sites

Overview

It is interesting how many military installations of one sort or another have left their mark on Cape Cod. Unfortunately, several have been totally removed, and in 2023 the National Park Service removed several more. They say that these were "...non-historic structures that are derelict and dilapidated..." I would disagree with the "non-historic" claim, but having been to these sites and have volunteered in one of the locations for several years and I must agree that they are dangerous and do pose serious health and safety threats.

We will cover two historic military sites. One was removed in 2023: the little known 6520th Air Control & Warning Squadron (Experimental) Radar Station in Truro, which was active during the early 1950s. Much of the second is still preserved: the 241st Coast Artillery Instillation that protected Cape Cod Canal during World War II. Two others that we won't be covering are the 762nd Radar Station in North Truro (now the home of the Payomet

Performing Arts Center) and Camp Wellfleet, a 1,738-acre training camp near Marconi Beach. Let's start with the 241st Coast Artillery Installation in Sagamore.

Cape Cod Canal

One of the most important features of Cape Cod is the Cape Cod Canal. Unless you flew onto the Cape or took a ferry from "the mainland," you had to go over one of the bridges crossing the Canal to get here. Construction of the Canal was started under private ownership in 1909 and was finally completed in the form we know today in 1940 after being updated and widened by the federal government after it took it over.

Trailhead to the 241st Coast Artillery Site

Talk of a canal across upper Cape Cod started way back in the 1620s in "Plimoth" Colony. At that time, the location held two rivers. One, the Scusset River, flowed northeast into Cape Cod Bay. The other, the Manomet River, flowed southwest into Buzzards Bay. The shortest distance between the two rivers was a bit over a mile, and the highest hill between them was only about thirty-three feet above sea level. If a Canal could be dug, it would facilitate trade between the Dutch in New York and Plimoth Colony and the Wampanoag Indians. Unfortunately, it was a prohibitively expensive project, even if the engineering and physical skills necessary had been available at that time. The first known survey and feasibility study for the Canal was completed in 1776 by an engineer with the Continental Army, Thomas Machin. This study, commissioned by General George Washington, surveyed the area to find out the feasibility of building a Canal to provide protection for the American Fleet from the British fleet and to prevent the British blockading Boston Harbor during the Revolutionary war (1775-1783).

Over the years, many companies were established to build the canal: in 1803, 1818, 1824, 1830, 1860, 1887 and again in 1899. Two of the most famous companies were the Cape Cod Ship Canal Company in 1887 and the Boston, Cape Cod, and New York Canal Company in 1899. August Belmont II, a wealthy banker (who built Belmont Park racetrack in New York and raised the racehorse Man o' War regarded by many as "the greatest racehorse of all time") purchased the Boston, Cape Cod, and New York Canal Company and reorganized it in 1904. He finally lifted the first shovelful of dirt in a ceremony in Bourne on June 22, 1909. The last dam (Foley's Dike) was removed on July 4, 1914, and the Cape Cod Canal was officially opened on July

29, 1914, beating the opening of the Panama Canal by seventeen days (August 15, 1914). President Woodrow Wilson ordered the Federal Railway Administration to operate the Canal during World War I. Belmont sold the canal to the federal government in 1927 for $11.5 million.

Foley's Dike Was Removed July 4, 1914 (Public Domain)

The Canal is thirty-two feet deep, four hundred eighty feet wide, and seven miles long, connecting Buzzards Bay in the south to Cape Cod Bay in the north.

The Canal in World War II

The canal was a very important seaway during World War II as it was an "inland" route for the movement of ships and cargo up the coast to Boston and beyond. This inland route became increasingly critical as the war progressed because German submarines began patrolling the Atlantic sea lanes very close to the shores of the United States. Even way back on July 21, 1918, during World War I, one such submarine (U-156) fired on a convoy of barges being pulled by a tugboat off of Orleans. The submarine managed to sink the barges and set the tug on fire. With this in mind, and with all the advances in German submarine technology, it was vitally important to keep ships away from the open ocean whenever possible, hence an inland route for shipping was imperative.

On December 8, 1941, war was declared on Japan, and on December 11, 1941 war was declared on Germany. Being at war with Germany made it necessary to beef up our coastal defenses along the East Coast. The army decided early on to set up gun emplacements to protect the canal. Two coastal artillery units, one at the Butler Point Military Reservation in Marion and one in Sandwich* at the Sagamore Hill Military Reservation, were constructed for this task.

To man the guns, they transferred Battery C of the 241st Coast Artillery Regiment of the Massachusetts National Guard from Deer Island in Winthrop to Sagamore. The job of the 241st was to protect the northern end of the Cape Cod Canal from a possible naval attack. The biggest worry again was from German submarines prowling along the Atlantic coast.

241st Gun Crew Ready for Action. Note Panama Mount.
(US Army Corps of Engineers)

There was good reason to worry. When one ship, the *SS Stephen R. Jones*, became grounded and sank, blocking the Canal on June 8,1942, ship traffic had to be diverted into the Atlantic and sent up around the northern tip of the Cape. Several weeks later, on July 3, 1942, a liberty ship, the *SS Alexander Macomb*, going around the tip carrying explosives, aircraft, and tanks to Russia was torpedoed and sunk by a German submarine *(U-215)* with the loss of ten sailors. The *Macomb*, on its maiden voyage, was not zigzaging and failed to keep up with the convoy because of heavy fog.

The *U-215* was also on her maiden voyage to lay mines in Boston Harbor. She was pursued by the *HMCS Le Tiger* and was sunk hours later on July 3, with all hands sealed inside. (*National Geographic* produced a television episode of *The Sea Hunters* [Season 5: Episode 5] entitled "U-215 & Alexander Macomb" which tells the story of the sinking of the *Macomb* and subsequent hunt for *U-215*.)

Entrances to the Underground Tunnels

The Sites

It is still possible to explore some of these eighty-plus-year-old defenses from World War II. One is just west of the Cape Cod Canal near Scusset Beach. There you can still find the remains of the 241st Coast Artillery installation at the Sagamore Hill Historic Site. The site is easy to find and contains several historical ruins and artifacts from a bygone era. Two hundred forty men were stationed there and were charged with patrolling the shore, watching for enemy airplanes, and preparing the guns for duty.

After walking a good distance from the "Sagamore Hill Historic Site" sign by the road, you will come to a clearing where you will see the openings to two Quonset hut-style, corrugated metal tunnels. These were the "Ready Room" entrances to a series of underground tunnels connecting ammunition storage rooms, coordinate plotting rooms, ammunition bunkers, and the two 155mm guns. The ends of the tunnels are blocked with wood now so it is not possible to enter more than a few yards. Just to the right of these tunnels, you will see a circular concrete gun pad called a Panama Mount on which a 155mm gun was mounted. Panama Mounts allowed the gunners to turn the gun in any direction with relative ease. From this area, you can continue a short distance up the hill to where the command station was located. The view from here is extraordinary. A short distance down the hill on the other side will bring you to the other Panama Mount where the second 155mm gun was located. These guns had a range of twenty miles and were affectionally named "Vicious Virgin" and "Big Mary."

155mm Gun "Vicious Virgin" (US Army Corps of Engineers)

The gun mounts, tunnel entrances, and battery commander's location are still visible. Each area has signage explaining in words and pictures exactly what was located at each position. The original installation was deactivated on April 1,1945. It's a nice hike, and you will see some interesting artifacts from a bygone era.

To Visit

Location: 20 Scusset Beach Road, Scusset Beach. A steep parking fee is charged from Memorial Day through October. Take Route 6 (Exit 1) east to Scusset Beach Road. You will pass the McDonald's on the south (canal) side of the road. Follow Scusset Beach Road straight through to the site. First, you will come to a parking lot where you will be charged for parking from May through October. Continue straight ahead for another short distance to the Visitor Center parking lot on the right. Cross the street and take the path next to the "Sagamore Hill Historic Site" sign. After you have finished your exploring you can take a walk through the Visitor Center to a nice promenade along the canal.

155mm Gun Panama Mount

*Names and locations can be confusing. The Sagamore Hill Historic Site is located on Sagamore Hill, which is located on the Scusset Beach State Reservation in Sandwich. (Most people don't realize that there is a little piece of Sandwich on the north side of the Canal.) Sagamore is the part of the town of Bourne bordering Sandwich east of Route 6 south of the Canal and east of Route 3 north of the Canal. Except for the small part in Sandwich, the Cape Cod Canal is located in the Town of Bourne. Most people think that Buzzards Bay is a town at the west end of the Canal. Sorry, like Sagamore to the East, Buzzards Bay is the part of the Town of Bourne at the west end of the Canal. I am confused, so you must be, too. You may want to look at a map!

2. BOURNE: THE KEITH CAR COMPANY AND THE GHOSTS OF SAGAMORE CEMETERY

Historic Sites

Ghosts and Ghouls and Mysterious Shapes

Overview

Did you know that there was a car company located in the village of Sagamore in Bourne? The plant was located on the north side of Route 6A. Didn't know that? At one time, this car company employed over 1,400 people and the actual buildings stretched on for over a mile. The longest structure was over 1,330 feet long–that's 3.7 football fields! Still nothing?

The Keith Car Company

The company was originally started by Isaac Keith and Ezekiel Ryder as a blacksmith shop in 1828. Along with doing work for the glass company in town, the company built sleighs and small buggies. Several years later Keith opened the Keith Car Works and eventually manufactured wheeled wagons and carriages. The company was in business in Sagamore through 1928. Never heard of it?

The Keith Car Manufacturing Company
(Courtesy of the Dennis Historical Society)

Not many people have heard of it, even though it was a rather large operation. Perhaps you were never in the market for a stagecoach, a carriage, a Conestoga wagon, picks and shovels, or maybe even a railroad freight or box car... no? A coffin, perhaps?

At one time or another the company made each of these items. Keith Car & Manufacturing was a prosperous company because it was able to change with the times. During the Gold Rush days (1848-1855), Keith Car & Manufacturing added axes, crowbars, picks, shovels, and other assorted tools to their wheeled product list, and during the Civil War (1861-1865) the company made specially reinforced wagons to carry Union cannons. They started making railroad freight cars in the late 1870s.

Most of the plant workers were immigrants from Italy, and for them the company created a factory town with over two dozen stores (and the first mall on Cape Cod) and homes. They even hired a company doctor and built a hospital for the community.

During World War I (1914-1918), Keith Car innovated again. This time, they manufactured 40,000 prefabricated box cars that they shipped to Marseille, France where they were assembled by German prisoners of war! A little-known fact is that Keith Car & Manufacturing designed and patented the famous 40-8 boxcar. 40-8? The boxcars could hold forty troops and eight horses! This boxcar was the backbone of troop, prisoner, and material movement from the late-1800s through World War I and II. (The troops could not have smelled very good after their travels with the horses… or the horses with their travels with the troops.)

The Keith Car Manufacturing Company Rail Siding (Courtesy of the Dennis Historical Society)

Keith Car saw an additional need and in the early 1900s they manufactured some coffins. The coffins were made to reinter bodies that had to be relocated when the Cape Cod Canal was being dug. More on this project below.

The company was bought by Standard Steel Car Company (SSC) in 1912 and continued production until it was closed in 1928. The buildings were torn down in 1930. Anything that remained was removed in the 1930s to make way for the widening of the Cape Cod Canal, which took place between 1935 and 1940. Interestingly, Standard Steel Car Company manufactured automobiles from 1913 until 1921, including over 2,300 Standard Steel Model E's in 1917 at a separate location. The company merged with Pullman Car and Manufacturing in 1934.

Keith Block, Plymouth Street, Sagamore
(Courtesy of the Dennis Historical Society)

Even though the Keith Car Plant is gone, many of the workers' houses still dot the area. These can be found from the ball park (Keith Field Recreation Area) on down Route 6A and even across the canal on Savary Avenue. In the early 1900's some boarding houses later evolved into the Canal View Apartments at the corner of Route 6A and Adams Street. A fire at the apartments in October 2016 destroyed a large section of one of the buildings causing over a million dollars damage.

Boarding House at Adams Street and Sandwich Road (1919)
(Courtesy of the Dennis Historical Society)

Sagamore Cemetery: Coffins and Mr. Keith

I mentioned above that there was a relationship between the Keith Car & Manufacturing Company and the Sagamore Cemetery. In reality there are two. First, the coffins: in 1909, during the digging of the Cape Cod Canal, sixty-two occupants from two local Bournedale burial grounds (forty-five from Emory Ellis Cemetery and seventeen from Collins Farm Cemetery) had to be relocated. As mentioned above, the Keith Car Works built the coffins. A seemly solid plan was developed to move the coffins and headstones. However, the best of plans sometimes don't turn out to be foolproof plans. As the headstones and occupants were removed from the two cemeteries, the names of the occupants were placed on the coffins (Part One of the foolproof plan).

Unfortunately, the names were written on the coffins in chalk (Part Two of the foolproof plan and Part One of its undoing). While the coffins awaited burial, the area was hit by a nor'easter (a very bad storm with heavy wind and rain), and the names of the occupants were partially or totally washed off (Part Two of the undoing of the foolproof plan)! The workers made their best guess about which coffin went with which headstone (Part Three of the undoing of the foolproof plan). The workers did their best...but not everyone was happy. Perhaps this even included the occupants! This brings us to the second relationship between the Keith Car & Manufacturing Company and the Sagamore Cemetery.

Digging the Cape Cod Canal (Public Domain)

Even before the mislabeled coffins were reinterred from the soon-to-be flooded cemeteries in the way of the Canal, the Sagamore Cemetery had been known for strange happenings. As long as anyone could remember, even well before 1909, townspeople and visitors to the cemetery reported hearing curious sounds, smelling unusual odors, and seeing ghostly apparitions in the cemetery. There were and still are reports of a ghost of a tall young man in a top hat and a tattered coat who vanishes when someone approaches him and an old woman who holds out her hands towards the visitors. Many believe that the man in the top hat is the ghost of a twenty-year-old man from the 1850s who is buried next to an eleven-year-old girl whose stone reads that she is his wife.

The Old Man Tree

Ah yes, there are also stories of the ghost of a girl of about eleven wearing a wedding dress and muddy leather boots roaming the cemetery. Some people relate stories of headstones being moved between their visits, as in the case of Eliza Howe's stone. It has fallen over and is currently leaning on the stone of Captain William Burgess, her husband. Captain Burgess was also a heavy cigar smoker and it is sometimes thought to be the cause of the strong cigar smell reported around an old tree found next to the road, a few hundred feet in from the cemetery's entrance. This old tree, when seen in profile, seems to look like the profile of an old man's face.

These strange occurrences are still being reported. One of the newer and most repeated narratives is by Donald Ellis whose relatives were among those reinterred during the 1909 move. Late in the day in July of 1998 as Mr. Ellis was clearing brush near the rear of the cemetery, he felt a sharp shove to his chest and smelled cigar smoke being blown into his face. It was a very hot afternoon, and Ellis reported that he stopped sweating, felt very cold, and developed goosebumps on his arms. He became extremely frightened. With further contemplation, Mr. Ellis concluded that the cigar smoking ghost who pushed him was most likely Isaac Keith, the founder of the Keith Car & Manufacturing Company and maker of the misidentified coffins. Ellis reported that several psychics who have since visited the cemetery have confirmed his interpretation of the event. It has been suggested that Mr. Keith continues to be very upset because many of the old Canal graves are not marked by the correct gravestones. The ghosts of Keith and the wrongly identified souls are believed to be some of the ones that have haunted the cemetery ever since the reburials.

Entrance to the Sagamore Cemetery

Many other visitors have also reported smelling cigar smoke by the old tree near the cemetery entrance. Donald Ellis and many other people believe that the area around the old tree is haunted by Emory Ellis where, with shotgun in hand, he protested the movement of his ancestor's remains (until he decided to take some money offered to him if he stopped his protest). Other visitors have taken photos containing unusual images and orbs, while others have reported feeling sudden blasts of cold air that they say have chilled them to the bone. This is truly a cemetery of lost and wandering souls trying to find their rightful and eternal resting place. I hope you don't get spooked when you go there. Please remember not to leave any traces of your visit or take any mementos (or residents) home with you.

To Visit

Location: On Route 6A just east of Route 6 Sagamore Bridge overpass. Exit 55 off of Route 6. South side of Sandwich Road (Route 6A), turn onto Ben Abbey Road. Entrance is on the right.

3. BARNSTABLE: THE GREAT HIDDEN BRICKWORKS

Historic Sites

Overview

The great brickworks in Barnstable is *almost* one of those "You can't get there from here!" places, as we New Englanders would say. You can get to it but finding it is difficult and could be a bit dangerous. I am including the brickworks in the book as a kind of "one up" for you if you know anyone in Barnstable. The Barnstable brickworks has an important place in the town's history, but it is a place that many long-time residents don't know much about or are not even aware of. I am talking about the West Barnstable Brick Company (WBBC).

The West Barnstable Brick Company in the Late 1880s (Public Domain)

I would rate WBBC right up there with the Keith Car Company with its mile long buildings in Sagamore as a famous location lost through the passage of time. The difference is that the Keith Car Company location is now under the waters of the Cape Cod Canal, and the remains of the WBBC are still here but are lost under a thick overgrowth and located in a difficult to get to location.

WBBC

The story started way back in 1878 when Noah Bradford, Jr., a direct descendent of Governor William Bradford of Plymouth Colony; Benjamin and Charles Crocker, whose dad manufactured shoes in Yarmouth Port; and Levi L. Goodspeed purchased nineteen acres of land in the Barnstable Great Marsh with the idea of creating a brick manufacturing company. This area was chosen because of the many large blue clay deposits found throughout the area. Several pottery businesses had been established in the area starting in 1820 because of these clay deposits. Interestingly, back in 1832 Noah Bradford's father opened his own pottery business there, which subsequently failed.

As with many new businesses, it was difficult at first, but that did not stop the foursome. In 1887, steam power was added to the factory, and several other structures were built. With this expansion, it was possible to manufacture two million bricks a year! It wasn't until 1888 when the company was bought by Cape Cod's legendary "Cranberry King" Abel D. Makepeace that the West Barnstable Brick Company finally prospered. Makepeace updated and added more new machinery, and to get enough workers to increase production, brought them in from Finland and Portugal. A year later, the company underwent another major extension.

Drying Bricks at the West Barnstable Brick Company in the late 1880s (Public Domain)

Interestingly, the A. D. Makepeace Company continues to be in business; however, their brickmaking operation is in the distant past. According to the company website, *"The A.D. Makepeace Company, based in Wareham, is the world's largest cranberry grower, the largest private property owner in eastern Massachusetts, and a recognized leader in environmentally responsible real estate development and stewardship."*

The Pits

The West Barnstable Brick Company location was ideal for making bricks, as the property had plenty of clay deposits to start with, and importantly, a railroad line running nearby. The only thing that was not available close by was wood for the kiln used to fire the bricks. The factory produced high-quality bricks in several steps. First, the clay was dug from pits around the property; second, the clay had to be cleaned of stones, sticks, roots, and other impurities; and finally, water was added and the slurry was poured into perfectly level brick molds. After that, the filled brick molds were fired or dried. Over the years, two sizes of bricks were manufactured: larger ones stamped "W.BARNSTABLE BRICK CO." and smaller ones stamped "W.B.B."

West Barnstable Brick Company became one of the premier Cape Cod businesses. During its heyday in the 1920s the factory could produce over 100,000 bricks a day or over thirty million bricks a year!

In October of 1925, the business was sold to Thomas Arden, a Taunton, Massachusetts insurance salesman who at one time ran the Gay Head Brick Company in Somerset. Mr. Arden improved the factory once again by adding a telephone and electric lights.

Unfortunately for Mr. Arden, this was the highpoint for the WBBC, and everything was downhill from that point. First, in 1928, President Herbert Hoover, hoping to have all building materials in the United States manufactured to a standard size, signed such a bill into law. Along with bricks, the law also standardized such commodities as eggs (sold by the dozen), milk (sold by the gallon), can sizes, screw sizes and threads, clothing, foods, and machinery.

One of the Few Standing Walls Remaining on the Site

Unfortunately, this was not good news for the West Barnstable Brick Company, which was now stuck with new equipment and a smoothly running manufacturing process revolving around the manufacture of bricks that were one-eighth of an inch (!!!) too short. The company had to scrap its old equipment, buy new replacement equipment, and subsequently raise brick prices because of these increased costs. This was all happening in 1933 just as the country was heading into the Great Depression. On top of that, to find out if all of these added costs could be recouped, in 1932 test holes were drilled in the clay pits to find out how much clay was left.

Management was very happy with the results of their query… at first. The answer was, "Yes, there should be enough clay available to continue manufacturing at or above the current production level for another fifty years." Unfortunatly, this good news lasted for only a very short time. Soon after the results of the drilling were made known, water started flowing up out of the holes drilled into the bottom of the clay pits, and all the pits flooded! The West Barnstable Brick Company, unable to afford the costs it would take to recover from this devastating event, had no choice but to go out of business.

That is the story of the West Barnstable Brick Company, how it became one of the biggest businesses on Cape Cod, and the unfortunate events that happened to end its life over the course of just a few short years. Now, after one hundred years, little of the company remains. If you do decide to look for it, all you will find are a few broken brick walls, pieces of broken bricks, and water-filled pits and holes.

Part of a Basement Wall at the Site

To Visit

Location: It is not the easiest place to get to. From Route 6, take Meetinghouse Way (Exit 65, Route 149) north to West Barnstable (Route 6A). Take a right onto Route 6A. Travel along Route 6A until you arrive at the location where a railroad track passes over the road. If you can find a place to park there you can walk easterly down the railroad track (check summer schedule for trains on this track) until you come across some overgrown paths on the bay (north) side of the track. As you walk down the track from this direction, you will walk over the Bridge Creek bridge. At that point, you will only be about a tenth of the way to the location.

Alternately, you could also continue driving down Route 6A until you come to Buttonwood Lane on the bay (north) side. Go down the lane, and at the end, there is a little circle where you may be able to park. It is only about twenty-five feet down a path to the railroad track. Go west (left) on the track. When you cross the Brickyard Creek bridge you will be about three quarters of the way to your destination.

Either way, you will have to walk just a small distance along the railroad track. (A factory manager was hit by a train and killed along the track in 1909. No ghost has been reported here, though.) If a train does come, you will have but three choices. First, you could get off the tracks and into the head-high briers and prickers lining the side of the track; second, you could get off the track and into one of the muddy bogs and third you could try to go down one of the very steep sides along some parts of the track. (I guess you also have a fourth choice.)

Eventually, you will come to a spot where you will find one of several 'paths' into the site on the bay (north) side of the track. You will have to plunge through the brush and downed trees for about 25 to 50 yards. These 'paths' are really overgrown. Please don't cut your own path. You will also find poison ivy, ticks, mud, and tripping hazards waiting for you.

4. BARNSTABLE: THE MOST HAUNTED JAIL IN AMERICA

Historic Sites

Ghosts and Ghouls and Mysterious Shapes

Overview

Here is a little story about something that was lost in time and discovered years later, just by accident. It is in the Town of Barnstable, and it is the oldest wooden jail (Old Gaol as it is called) in the United States. The jail was built sometime around 1690 by order of the Massachusetts Bay Colony and Massachusetts Bay Colony courts. Amazingly, Old Gaol was designed to house only six prisoners. Since bail was not something easily obtained (it was an extreme exception), overcrowding was the rule and not the exception.

Even though the Barnstable County sheriff was in charge of the jail, the day-to-day running was left to non-paid jail-keepers who made their "pay" by selling food and goods to the prisoners. Prisoners were allowed to beg for money to pay the jailers for food, blankets, and other needs. Many of the incarcerated died from cold, abuse, hunger, or disease in overcrowded and windowless cells where prisoners were not even segregated by age, sex, illness, or crime.

The Barnstable County Historical Society Website lists "criminals" including "…rogues, vagabonds, beggars, jugglers *(Author Note: a wizard, conjurer, magician, or one who obtains things through fraudulent means)*, fortune tellers, runaways, stubborn servants or children, pilferers, wanton and lascivious persons, and common railers *(Author Note: someone who overly objects or criticizes, uses abusive language, or tells vulgar jokes)* and brawlers." Wealthy and well-connected inmates often bribed the jailers and sheriff and were allowed to live comfortably in private homes around Barnstable Village.

The Old Gaol

Old Gaol

Old Gaol was the Barnstable County jail until a new stone jail was built in 1820. Originally, Old Gaol stood alone on Old Jail Lane in Barnstable, but it was later incorporated into the barn built to house the town Constable's horse. Not much is known about the Old Gaol for the next one-hundred-forty-eight years. It just sat in obscurity as part of a barn on Old Jail Lane. In 1968, it was rediscovered still attached to the barn. Old Gaol was then separated from the barn, dismantled into moveable parts, and transported to the Coast Guard Heritage Museum parking lot. Interestingly, the Coast Guard Heritage Museum at one time was the old customshouse (1856-1913) building!

The jail has the appearance of a small, white, two-story house stuck in the back of the sunken parking lot. It is not much wider than the two windows on the second floor. In 1971, Old Gaol was finally added to the National Register of Historic Places. Old Gaol and the former customshouse can be found near the corner of Millway and Main Street (Route 6A) on Cobbs Hill in Barnstable.

Famous Prisoners

Even though the jail was originally constructed to house common debtors and inmates awaiting trial and/or sentencing, over the years many famous and infamous prisoners were housed there, as well. Probably the most famous person to be jailed there was Goody Hallett (AKA Mehitable, Mariah, Maria Hallett, the Witch of Wellfleet and the Witch in the Red Shoes), the lover of the famed pirate Black Samuel Bellamy, who also had another connection to Old Gaol.

On April 26, 1717, Black Sam's ship, the *Whydah Gally*, was blown aground, torn apart, capsized, and sank around midnight during a terrible nor'easter off the coast of Wellfleet. Black Sam (this name was really "given" to him about 100 years later) probably did not survive the sinking. The bodies of one-hundred-four of his crew were washed ashore with forty-two pirates unaccounted for but believed drowned. At least two members of the crew (the *Whydah Gally*'s pilot and a ships carpenter) and a sixteen-year-old Miskito Indian cabin boy survived and were arrested along with seven survivors of Black Sam's consort ship the *Mary Anne*. The "consort ship" carried the wives, children, and partners of the pirates on board the *Whydah Gally*. The *Mary Anne* went down that same night several miles south of the *Whydah Gally* near Pochet Island in Orleans.

Second Floor Jail Cells at the Old Gaol
(Courtesy of the Barnstable Historical Society)

All nine of the survivors from both ships were captured and arrested by Justice Joseph Doane and were then jailed in the Old Gaol. They were later brought to trial for piracy in Boston. Six of the inmates were convicted on October 22, 1717, and were rowed across Boston Harbor to Charlestown, where they were hanged on November 15. On their last trip, they were accompanied by the famous Puritan Minister Cotton Mather who said that they all confessed and repented for their crimes on the trip over to the gallows. Those hanged included Thomas Baker of the Netherlands, John Brown of Jamaica, Peter Cornelius Hoff of Sweden, Hendrick Quainter also of the Netherlands, John Shaun of France, and Simon Van Der Vorst of New York. Pirate ships were like mini United Nations! Unfortunately for the condemned, King George had pardoned all the pirates two months earlier (on September 8th), but the pardon arrived in Boston too late to save them. Two of the other nine inmates were set free and one, the sixteen-year-old Miskito Indian cabin boy, was sold into slavery.

The Ghosts

The jail is considered one of the most haunted buildings in America. From the above description of the conditions in the jail, it is not difficult to see why. Legend has it that Goody Hallett and several other former inmates still haunt the jail. (See the article "Wellfleet: The Ghost of Goody Hallett" for more information on Goody.) At certain times of the year, ghost tours are given. Around Halloween the Old Goal ghost tour is particularly creepy.

The Old Gaol (far left) and the Customshouse (right)

The Customshouse next door was designed by Ammi Your and built in 1855 along with a carriage house that is located next to it. The building was used as a Customshouse and local post office until 1913. It continued as the post office until 1958 and repurposed as a museum in 1960. The building was listed in the National Register of Historic Places in 1975.

To Visit

Location: 3365 Main Street, Barnstable. East end of town on the south side of Main Street (Route 6A). It is just to the left of the Coast Guard Heritage Museum. Coast Guard Heritage Museum is a large red brick building near the road. The sunken parking lot is to the left of the Museum. The Jail is stuck in the back right corner of this parking lot. It was surrounded by old cars the last time I was there.

The Jail is open Saturdays from the third week in June until the second week in October (check the dates to be sure) from noon until 2 pm. Donation as I write this is only $5.

5. DENNIS:
THE PRINCESS OF SCARGO TOWER AND THE OLD INDIAN BURIAL GROUND

Legends and Lore

Overview

There are many beautiful scenic overlooks and views on Cape Cod. Some are hard to hike to or even find. Here is a very easy one. One of the nicest and often unnoticed panoramic views is from Scargo Tower in Dennis. On a clear day you can see all the way from Provincetown to Plymouth. It even overlooks a pond in the shape of a fish! The tower is an easy climb since it is only thirty feet high and the kids will love the visit and climb because they feel like they are climbing the tower of a real castle. You are probably thinking, "How can we see such a great distance from a tower only thirty feet high?" I am glad you asked. The tower is located on Scargo Hill, one of the best-known and highest (160 feet) hills on Cape Cod. Don't worry, the parking lot is at the base of the tower, not at the base of the hill!

Scargo Tower

The Observatory

The original tower was made of wood and built in 1874 by Charles Humphrey as a way of attracting tourists to his nearby "luxury" hotel, the three-story, fifty-room, French-empire style Cape Cod Bay House that he had recently bought from James Lufkin. Mr. Lufkin bought the Minot House in Scituate in 1870, had it dismantled, and floated it to Dennis. Here he rebuilt it on a sixty-foot hill overlooking Cape Cod Bay. He also changed its name from Minot House to Cape Cod Bay House to better match its new location and help attract tourists. Soon after Mr. Lufkin completed the rebuild, he sold it to Mr. Humphrey, who reopened it in 1873. The following year, Mr. Humphrey built a tower observatory, which some call the "first" Scargo Tower.

The Cape Cod Bay House was located on 125 acres at the end of Nobscussett Road near what is now Bay View Beach. According to the Dennis Historical Society Newsletter (June 2017), *"Bathing, boating, fishing, rambling, croquet, lawn tennis, swings, an ice house, and a 'never fail' spring were advertised."*

The property changed hands again. This time Charles Tobey, who founded Tobey Furniture Company in Chicago, purchased the Cape Cod Bay House in 1885 and renamed it the Nobscussett House (after the Nobscussett Tribe that lived in the area). Tobey added a dance hall, bowling alley, billiard room, an additional story and a half to the building, bathing pavilions, a pier, and a string of guest cottages. Eventually the complex included tennis courts and a golf course and covered 215 acres.

The observatory became known near and far as the "Tobey Tower." Unfortunately, the original tower was blown down in a wind storm in 1886. A second wooden tower was built in its place, but this one was also not meant to be. It burned to the ground in 1900. A third tower was then built. Having learned from past mistakes, this one was built of cobblestones and was reopened in 1901.

The stock market crash in 1929 and the depression that followed caused the Nobscussett Hotel to close its doors. In 1930, the hotel was torn down and most of the land was sold off. The hill and tower were given to the town of Dennis. There is a plaque above the entrance to the tower that reads: *"This tower and hilltop were given to the town of Dennis in 1929 in memorial to Charles Tobey (1831-1888) and Francis Bassett Tobey (1833-1913). Loyal sons of the village of Dennis where their Tobey ancestors settled in 1678."*

Scargo Lake

Now, let's return to the fish-shaped Scargo Lake and the legend that accompanies it. There are several versions of the lake's origin, including one of the lake being formed by the ancient Wampanoag giant god, Maushop, who also created Martha's Vineyard and Nantucket. As a thank-you offering for making Martha's Vineyard, Maushop was given all the tobacco on the island. After smoking it all, he knocked the dottle (the remains of ash and tobacco) out of his pipe. The dottle landed in the water nearby, and thus Nantucket Island was formed!

A View of Scargo Lake from Scargo Tower with Cape Cod Bay in the Distance

The legend most repeated, though, concerns Scargo, a Native American princess of the Nobscussett tribe. Many years ago, Princess Scargo fell in love with Weaquaquet, a young brave from a nearby tribe. Weaquaquet gave his beloved Princess a pumpkin containing four baby fish. Princess Scargo did not want them to perish, so she built a small pond to keep them in.

Weaquaquet went off to battle soon after but promised to return by the time the fish had grown. Upon awakening one morning, Princess Scargo found that the pond had dried up and three of the fish had died. She cried so hard that the little pond rapidly filled with her tears, and the one remaining fish miraculously survived. Seeing what had happened, her father Chief Sagem ordered the princess's handmaidens to gather some clamshells and scoop out a larger pond for the fish, the dimensions of which were marked by arrows shot by a brave from the tribe. Legend has it that the dirt and sand that the handmaidens scooped out were piled on the shore, forming the hill that Scargo Tower sits on.

Waequaquet returned just before the fish was fully grown, and he and Princess Scargo were subsequently married. The princess and the brave lived on the shore of Scargo Lake, and the descendants of that one fish can still be found swimming in the lake.

Remembrances Left at the Burial Ground

Legend has it that the happy couple leave their graves (said to be in the Nobscussett Indian Burial Ground on Old Kings Highway [Route 6A]) to enjoy warm evenings together sitting and strolling along the shores of Scargo Lake. It is said that sometimes they can be seen contentedly sitting on the granite and iron fence surrounding the Burial Ground. Incidentally the fence was erected by the Town of Dennis in 1829 for a cost of $129.

There are no signs to the Burial Ground save one on Route 6A pointing to a partially hidden tree-covered path leading to the area. There is also a carved stone at the end of the path that reads: *"Burial Ground of the Nobscussett Tribe of Indians of which Tribe Mashantampaine was Chief."* Aside from the partially hidden path and the aforementioned stone and iron fence, there are no headstones or grave markings, no paths through the cemetery, no attendants, and no parking lot.

When the leaves are off the trees, there is a nice view of Scargo Lake from the iron posts at the far end of the cemetery. In groupings around the grounds and on the cement benches, you will find curios and oddities, dollar bills and loose change, dream catchers, ribbons, figurines, and other knickknacks left by friends and strangers for the Burial Ground's spirits and inhabitants. Please enjoy them, perhaps leave something of your own, but leave the rest of the gifts and offerings undisturbed.

To Visit

Location: Scargo Tower: Scargo Hill Road, South Dennis off of Old King's Highway (AKA Main Street, Route 6A). Take Exit 78 off Route 6 and follow Massachusetts Route 134 North. When you reach Route 6A (about 3 miles) take a left. After .4

miles turn left onto Scargo Hill Road. Go .7 miles and turn right on Dr. Stanton Road.

The Nobscussett Burial Grounds are found west on Old King's Highway across from Osprey Lane which is on the north side of 6A. There is a small parking area about thirty feet in on the right on Osprey Lane. It is not easy to find the entrance to the Burial Grounds, which is located behind the homes on the south side of Route 6A. Directly across from Osprey Lane is a stone wall. Entrance to the Grounds is about fifteen feet to the right of the wall. It is a long path covered by a beautiful canopy of trees.

6. CHATHAM AND WELLFLEET: THE MARCONI STATION SITES

Historic Sites

Overview

As you sit reading this book, you probably have a cell phone within arm's reach. With this you can instantly call a friend no matter where you or they are, you can call and have a pizza delivered to your door–well not where I live in North Truro, or if you are in peril: fire, police or medical attention are just three taps away. You can also check my 'facts', though I am sure that you would not even think of doing that. By the way, did you know that the first cellular phones were invented on April 3, 1973? It was not until June of 2007 when the iPhone (with a 3.5-inch screen) was released that they really took off. Yes, I know, the BlackBerry was released in January of 1999, but it did not cause the frenzy that the iPhone did. Half of the people reading this are saying, "What the heck is a BlackBerry?" (Let's just say that it was a very popular interactive pager in the mid-1990s that later morphed into a smartphone.)

Such instant verbal communication was not the case for most of human existence. Probably some of the earliest documented transmission of messages were by smoke, drumbeats, or signal fires used by the early Egyptians, Greeks, and Chinese. Unfortunately, you had to be able to see or hear these and that, along with weather, was severely limiting.

Another line-of-sight method that was developed in 1790 was the semaphore. This was a series of high towers built on hilltops that had movable arms used to spell out a message. Crews were even given telescopes to increase their visual acuity. Using roughly the same arm positions, the US Navy still uses semaphore signaling with or without flags (to increase visibility) between ships at sea at certain times!

It was not until the telegraph was invented in 1837 that words could be transmitted great distances...but just over wires and just by Morse Code, which is a series of long and short clicks for each letter in each word. Voice could finally be transmitted thanks to Alexander Graham Bell in 1876. Unfortunately, Bell also needed wires to carry the voice from one location to another.

Marconi and Radio

Society could finally free itself of wired communications in 1895 when radio was invented. It was still "wireless telegraphy," though: just a series of dots and dashes from one location to another. Wireless communication was first developed and accomplished by Guglielmo Marconi, an Italian inventor. Marconi sent a wireless signal across the English Channel four years later in 1899, and in 1901 the letter "S" (three dots) was telegraphed from England to Newfoundland.

The human voice was first transmitted on December 23, 1900, between two 50-foot towers on Cobb Island in the Potomac River in Washington, DC, by Reginald Fessenden using equipment he had developed. He also broadcast the first 'radio program' on Christmas Eve in 1906. It was a Christmas Concert. First, Fessenden introduced the concert, next a recording of Hendel's *Largo* was played, followed by Fessenden playing *O Holy Night* on his violin, and finally he said, "Goodnight to all" and signed off.

The first transatlantic wireless communication took place on January 18, 1903. It was a simple greeting between Britain's King Edward VII and United States President Theodore Roosevelt. This message was sent from the Marconi Station right here in Wellfleet.

Marconi became interested in "wireless telegraphy," (the transmission of messages without wires) at a very young age and actually demonstrated radio transmission when he was twenty to his mother in December of 1894. He placed a simple transmitter on one side of the room and made a bell ring on the other side. Through simple experimentation in 1895, he found that if he used a taller antenna, he could transmit over hills to a receiver two miles away. In March of 1897 he stretched this to 3.7 miles and on the 13th of May of 1897, he managed 9.9 miles.

First US Wireless Station

Marconi first started his search for a perfect place to build a wireless station in the United States in 1900. The ideal location had to be near labor, building supplies, water, a hotel, and a rail line. He searched all along the New York, Connecticut, Rhode Island, and Massachusetts coast. In February of 1901, Marconi finally arrived in Provincetown. Ed Cook, a local, took him around the area in his wagon. Marconi decided that the best spot for his station was the Highland Light area in North Truro. Unfortunately for Marconi (and Truro), the locals thought he was a fraud and a quack and refused to sell him the land.

Location of the Original Marconi Site Antenna Field in Wellfleet

Cook then took Marconi to South Wellfleet and showed him an eight-acre piece of land he just happened to own. It was on top of a 130-foot cliff and had a railroad station, telegraph office, and harbor nearby. Marconi bought the piece of land and hired Cook as the general contractor. He told Cook to build a station that included a transmitter building, a kerosene engine housing, cottages, and an array of twenty 200-foot-tall towers. His antenna wires were strung over and between the tops of these towers.

By 1902 there were wireless stations in Wellfleet; Grace Bay, Nova Scotia, Canada; and Poldhu, Cornwall, England. Unfortunately, in late November 1902 a storm hit Wellfleet and knocked down the masts. Marconi decided to rebuild just four 210-foot towers to support his antennae. The new configuration was up and running by January of 1903. When the station was first used, it set off a deafening sharp crack and a spark that was said could be seen four miles away.

Electricity finds any way it can to get to the ground. At the Marconi station, this could be stove pipes, drainpipes, and even the clotheslines. The housekeeper at the station once said that she got used to getting a shock whenever she hung out clothes.

As mentioned above, President Roosevelt and King Edward VII exchanged greetings in January of 1903. You can visit the site near Marconi Beach in Wellfleet. Most of the station is gone now. It was partially removed during World War I for security reasons and most of what was left of the site washed away by erosion many years ago. Some remnants of the station may still be seen, though.

The New Station

After building a huge station in Siasconset on Nantucket, Marconi decided he had to move the Wellfleet station because of all the wind and erosion at its present location. The building of the new station was started in 1914 and was finally finished in 1920. It was built in two locations, with transmitters in Marion, Massachusetts, and receivers in Chatham. The station was located along Ryder Cove in Chatham and was composed of fifteen buildings spread over 104 acres. During this period, World War I intervened, and the equipment needed for the Chatham station could not be shipped from England, the site of the Marconi parent company's manufacturing operations. When the station was finally finished in the 1920s, most of Marconi's equipment was obsolete, and the station was taken over by RCA (Radio Corporation of America). Ship-to-shore transmissions started in April, 1921. The Chatham station finally closed in 1997. It is now the Chatham Marconi Maritime Center on Route 28.

Path to the Antenna Field at the Chatham Marconi Site

The original Chatham station had six 360-foot towers, five of which were removed in 1919. The sixth was finally removed in 1956. At one time, this was the largest ship-to-shore radio telegraph station in the United States, and during World War II it was the nerve center for monitoring Nazi U-boat messages in the Atlantic. The site has an interesting museum and behind it, an Antenna Field Trail (over 650 feet long) leading to the top of a hill where you can see the base of one of the six 360-foot tall antennae and also have an enjoyable view of Stillwater Pond. Interestingly, these six antennae stretched for over a mile and pointed directly at Stavanger in Norway.

In the early 1900's most ships at sea had a Marconi installation staffed with Marconi Company employees. This equipment is credited with getting help to the Titanic survivors on the morning of April 15, 1912.

To Visit

Location: The Wellfleet Marconi Wireless site is accessed by taking Marconi Beach Road off of Route 6. It is on the East (ocean) side and can't be missed since the road is the entrance way to Marconi Beach. Take your first left (Marconi Station Road). Before proceeding to the parking lot at the end of the road you should stop at the National Park Service Office on the left. It contains wonderful information and photos of the Marconi Station, including a detailed model, so you can get a good idea of the vastness of the project. Once you get to the parking lot at the end of the road, follow the trail up to the observation deck.

The Chatham Marconi Wireless Receiving Station is on the corner of Orleans Road (MA28) and Old Comers Road. Don't forget to walk up the Antenna Field Trail behind the museum.

7. ORLEANS: THE GHOSTS OF ORLEANS WATERFRONT INN

Legends and Lore

Overview

I love an old ghost story, especially one that intertwines factual local history and a ghost or ghosts of real people in real places. The "ghosts of the Orleans Waterfront Inn" is one such story. It contains one historic family who still run a popular and prosperous business today, one old home/hotel/inn that has been resurrected as a wonderful restaurant and hotel, a wash-a-shore family who made the latter possible, and four (or five) friendly ghosts.

A Captain's Home

If you have ever headed out of the Stop and Shop parking lot on Route 6A in Orleans, you can't miss the Orleans Waterfront Inn. It looms high across the street, a stately old building that is worth a visit. Here you will find a cozy Irish Pub, a wonderful waterfront dining room, a relaxing deck overlooking the cove, and eleven beautiful guest rooms. It is a wonderful location for weddings venues and events with up to two hundred guests. Oh, and did I mention the three (or four) permanent residents? That is where the ghosts come in.

What is currently the Inn was built in 1875 by Sea Captain Aaron Snow as a home for his wife and seven children. It was built tall so that Arron's wife would be the first in town to see her husband's ship come home. Behind the Inn, just about where the back deck is located, Aaron built a wharf to berth his schooner, the *Nettie M Rogers*. The wharf was built of wood from the many shipwrecks that happened along the Nauset Shoals. It is sad that none of it remains today.

From his wharf, Snow sailed all over New England to purchase goods, fuels, and grain that he brought back to sell in Orleans in the store on the first floor of his home and in several surrounding out buildings. Aaron's son, William, moved the business to the center of Orleans where it continues to be run by the Snow family. Aaron Snow died on the 10th of May, 1892. By that time the home he built was just an empty old building that was known affectionally as "Aaron's Folly" by the locals.

The Orleans Waterfront Inn

The building remained empty until it was finally purchased eight years later in 1900. Up until the beginning of World War II, the building was run as a boarding house and had at least four different owners. I should be a little more technically correct: in the 1920s the "boarding house" was said to have been run not as a boarding house but rather as a house of ill repute. After World War II the southwest and northeast wings were added. At that time, the building was initially only open as a summer inn and then later converted into a year-round hotel.

The Inn

Ed Maas bought the hotel in 1996 and continues to own it to this day. Originally, he was going to tear the then-deserted building down but one day after walking through the inn, his wife said that he had to save the building for the ghosts! (Wait—where did the ghosts come from?)

There are numerous stories about different ghosts frequenting the Inn. Some stories are a bit muddled, confusing, and complicated. According to a few of the "stories," four (or five) ghosts occupy the Inn and the surrounding area. We have the "Old Spinster" who owned the Inn at the turn of the 20th century; "Hannah" a "working girl" during the roaring 1920s who was said to be murdered near the front entrance to the Inn; "Fred" a bartender who hung himself in the cupola in the 1950s; and "Paul" a dishwasher who hung himself in the basement in the 1970s. Got that? "Old Spinsters," "Hannah," "Fred," and "Paul." There is even another story of a young boy who appears in a nearby garden. Luckily, they all seem to be friendly.

The most notable ghost is Hannah, the *file de joie* who was murdered by a customer at the entrance. Owner Maas claims that he saw her one night as he was falling sleep on the couch. He glanced over and saw a naked woman walk into the room. He said he did not think very much of what he thought he saw (really?), believing it was just a dream. However, he was awakened several minutes later when he received a phone call from a passing motorist. The motorist asked Maas to put curtains up on the fifth-floor windows because a naked woman was dancing in the room. Maas was taken aback by this since there were no guests staying on the fifth floor that night.

It seems that Hannah, who lives in Room 5, is a friendly ghost, often opening doors, lighting candles, and dancing *au naturel*. She is reportedly one of the Inn's regulars. The SyFy channel produced a *Ghost Hunters* episode about the Inn and Hannah. SyFy called the Inn "The Inn of the Dead." (I believe you can access a video of this show on YouTube.) I would not let any of this dissuade you from stopping by to enjoy a meal or some libation at the bar or even from staying at the Inn if you are in the area. You will enjoy yourself and you may even meet some interesting "guests"… remember, however, Hannah's dance card fills quickly!

In the earlier years of ownership, Maas played up the ghost stories but has since been downplaying the ghost stories and instead up-playing the Orleans Waterfront Inn as an upscaled Inn.

To Visit

Location: Orleans Waterfront Inn: Take route 6 to the Orleans/ Eastham Rotary. Exit at Route 6A West. Go 100 feet and turn left onto Old Country Road.

Snow's Home and Garden: Take Route 6A (AKA Cranberry Highway or Old King's Highway) into Orleans. Go North on

Main Street for 500 feet and you will see *Snow's* Home and Garden "Family owned and operated since 1887" on the right.

8. EASTHAM: INDIAN ROCK AND THE WONDERS OF FORT HILL

Historic Sites

Overview

One of the most beautiful locations on Cape Cod is the Fort Hill area of Eastham. If you just want to hike through a beautiful area by the sea, this is one of those special places. There are spectacular views of Nauset Marsh, wonderful paved trails through grassy and wooded areas, and a connection to the boardwalk on the Red Maple Swamp Trail. Don't be surprised if you see artists painting the marvelous views and parents, grandparents, children, and lovers walking the trails and enjoying the peace and tranquility of the area as perhaps they investigate and enjoy the numerous plants, insects, birds, and views of the area.

As with other parts of Cape Cod, there are links throughout the area joining decades, centuries, or millennia to geologic and human history. You just have to know where to find them and what they mean.

Indian Rock

The Community Stone

Members of the Nauset Tribe of the Wampanoag have lived in the Fort Hill area and Cape Cod for thousands of years, and artifacts of their existence can be found in many locations here and around the Eastham area. One interesting artifact you should take a look at is a giant grinding stone. There are several such stones in Massachusetts; however, the one best and most frequently visited on Cape Cod is the one known as "Indian Rock," located at Fort Hill.

Well Worn Grooves Left From Sharpening Tools

Indian Rock is one of four grinding stones found in the Nauset area. It is made of a fine grain metamorphic rock and was used by the Nauset people to grind or sharpen stone that they used for axes, arrowheads, cutting tools, and pieces of bone out of which they fashioned fish hooks and pins. Over the centuries, deep grooves, channels, and indentations have worn into the rock by the Nauset people as they sharpened and shaped their utensils and tools: the axes in the deeper grooves and the fish hooks and bone in the narrower grooves.

This particular stone was a "community stone" used by all members of the tribe. The rock was found in the mud just below where it is displayed on Skiff Hill. The National Park service moved the twenty-ton rock to its present location soon after taking over this land in 1965. They also built a wonderful little pavilion and a marker describing the stone, along with drawings of some of the implements the Nauset people may have sharpened or polished on this very rock.

Indian Rock is most easily accessed from Hemenway Road off Route 6 on the east (ocean) side of Fort Hill.

Samuel Treat

There are other artifacts of historical importance at Fort Hill. You may want to either walk down the trail from Indian Rock in the direction of the south Fort Hill Trail parking lot or drive south to that parking lot (directions below).

A few hundred feet along the trail, northeast of the Fort Hill Trail parking lot, is a granite post. Most people walk past this two-foot-high post every year without giving it a second glance. Very few others may have spotted but disregarded a lone letter "T" carved into its southwest facing side.

Northern Boundary Property Marker of Pastor Treat's Property

This lone post marks the northern boundary of a 20-acre parcel of land owned by Pastor Samuel Treat in the 1600s. Samuel Treat was an interesting individual, as well as a famous historical figure from Cape Cod's past. He was born in Milford, Connecticut, on September 3, 1648. Upon his graduation from Harvard University, he was assigned to be a minister to an assembly of Puritans and the indigenous people in Eastham. He was paid 50 pounds, part of the "oyle" from every whale that was brought ashore, and "sufficient wood" brought to his home for heating and cooking.

Treat was married twice, first to Elizabeth Mayo on March 16, 1674, with whom he had ten surviving children. Elizabeth died on December 4, 1696. Is it any wonder? He subsequently married Abigail Willard on August 29, 1700, with whom he had two children.

Treat was noted for his "hellfire and damnation" style of preaching, and it was said that his preaching could be heard far from the meetinghouse even during howling winds and storms*.

In his efforts to convert the Nauset people to Christianity he became very involved with the tribe. He attended many of their cultural events and learned to fluently speak their native (Massachusetts or Algonquin) language. It is said that he was befriended and so respected by the Nauset people that when he died they actually dug a tunnel through a snow drift to his front door so they could move his body to the meetinghouse.

When he died, each of the ten children from his first wife received 5 shillings (about 31 cents today). The two children from his second wife split the remainder of his estate, which came to less than 50 shillings. Being a minister has never been a money-making profession (unless perhaps you are on television).

He died on March 18, 1716, and was buried in the Cove Burying Ground on Route 6 just south of Corliss Way in Eastham. His original slate gravestone was stolen in the 1800s, and a marble one was put in its place. In the early 1900s the original gravestone was found in a barn in Orleans and was not returned to Eastham but placed in the Snow Library in Orleans for safekeeping. Unfortunately, this did not work out as planned. Snow Library and the original gravestone were destroyed in a fire in 1952. The second stone is currently located back where it belongs at the Cove Burying Ground.

The following is inscribed on the original gravestone:

HERE LYES INTERRED
Ye BODY OF Ye LATE LEARNED &
REVd Mr SAMUEL TREAT
Ye PIOUS & FAITHFUL PASTOR OF THIS CHURCH
WHO AFTER A VERY ZEALOUS DISCHARGE OF
HIS MINISTRY
FOR Ye SPACE OF 45 YEARS &
A LABORIOUS TRAVEL FOR Ye SOULS OF Ye INDI-
AN NATIVES
FELL ASLEEP IN CHRIST MARCH Ye 18 1716/17
IN Ye 69 YEAR OF HIS AGE

The replacement simply says:

REV
SAMUEL TREAT
DIED
MAR 18, 1716
AGED 69 YEARS

A Trail and a Whaler

While you are visiting Fort Hill, you might want to take advantage of some of the other sites. Two of which are the Red Maple Swamp Trail boardwalk and the restored home of Edward Penniman, a famous whaling captain.

The Red Maple Swamp Trail can be accessed near Indian Rock or just up the trail from the Treat property boundary marker. The trail is only about .8 miles round trip and will take just a little over thirty minutes, that is if you don't stop to take in the views. It has a neat boardwalk section that winds through the heart of the swamp. Of course, red maples can be stunning in the fall. Pets are not allowed on the trail.

If you enter the Fort Hill area from the south off of Route 6 by way of Governor Prence Road/Fort Hill Road, you will pass the Penniman House. That Second Empire style house is on the right, and you sure can't miss it. Just by looking at it you will want to go in and have a look around.

The house was built by a successful whaler, Captain Edward Penniman, in 1868. Captain Penniman died on October 15, 1913 at the age of 82. He is buried in the Evergreen Cemetery in Eastham across from *Arnolds Lobster and Clam Bar*. The Captain's youngest granddaughter sold the house to the National Park Service in 1963 for $28,000. (That is about $275,000 in 2020 money.) Thank you for this piece of history! In 1976 it was placed in the National Register of Historic Places. The NPS runs it as a museum and has done a wonderful job restoring the home and grounds.

To Visit

Location: 200 Hemenway Road, Eastham. Route 6 to Hemenway Road on the east (ocean) side. Drive 0.3 miles to the parking at the end of the road. This is a town parking lot and requires a town parking permit. Parking may be available on both sides of the road leading to the parking lot. Obey any road signs. Just before the parking lot you will see the path on the right (south) side of the road. Take this about 0.1 miles to Indian Rock. You may want to continue 0.1 miles up the path to the Fort Hill area. It is a large open expanse with several hiking trails and great views.

Alternatively, you can hike here from the Fort Hill Trail parking area at the south end of the Fort Hill area. To get to the Fort Hill Trail parking lot, take Route 6 (south) to Governor Prence Road on east (ocean) side. Go east on Governor Prence Road. It will turn into Fort Hill Road. The Fort Hill parking lot is on your left. The trail to Indian Rock and Pastor Treat's land marker is at the northeast corner of the parking lot.

*Samual Treat [1648-1716], Familypedia, https://familypedia.fandom.com/wiki/Samuel_Treat_(1648-1716)

9. EASTHAM: FIRST ENCOUNTER BEACH MONUMENT?

Historic Sites

Overview

American history devotees from all over the country make their way to a plaque on a stone at the south end of the parking lot at First Encounter Beach in Eastham. Stand near it for a while. You will notice that most other people just walk by the stone without giving it a second glance. Years ago, I remember overhearing a local tell a tourist that the name came from an old Indian legend about an alien encounter at the beach. The tourist thought that the local was pulling his leg but, surprisingly… and honestly, he wasn't.

Wait a minute. That might be the First Encounter Beach *parking lot* monument, but it is not the *original* First Encounter Beach Tercentenary Memorial placed in 1920. The *parking lot* plaque most people look at and take photographs of (well not really—as I said, most people just walk past with nary a glance) was installed in 2001 and not in 1920 as the original one was. The 2001 plaque is not much to look at. It's just a smallish square rock next to a bike rack near the edge beach. So where is the original monument? Let's find out.

New Monument (Tiny Black Square Above the Cars)

The First Encounter?

First, we should review a little history. As you may remember from your American History course, the Mayflower's original destination was the Hudson River, which was at that time part of the Virginia Colony. However, the little boat was blown off course and landed in (drumroll, please), no, not Plymouth, but Provincetown on November 21 (O.S. November 11), 1620. Remember what we said at the beginning of the book about dates.

On December 8, 1620, a band of sixteen Pilgrims in search of food made their way by boat down to somewhere near where First Encounter Beach is located. After coming ashore and exploring for a short time, one of the men started yelling "Indians, Indians," or really *"Indeans, Indeans,"* just as a volley of arrows rained down on their little party. Some of the Pilgrims were able to return to their small boat to retrieve their firearms and fired at the *Indeans*. Understanding that retreat is the better part of valor, the *Indeans* melted into the woods. So you see, to the *Indeans* these wash-a-shores were "aliens."

..."Men, Indeans, Indeans", and with All, their arowes came flying amongst them. Their men ran with all speed to recover their armes, as by ye good providence of God they did... The crie of ye Indeans was dreadfull, espetially when they saw ther men rune out of ye randevoue towourds ye shallop... they soon got their armes, & let flye amongs them, and quickly stopped their violence... Aterwards they gave God sollamne thanks & praise for their deliverance... *

This was the Pilgrims first encounter with the indigenous inhabitants and hence the name of the beach. This was probably not the indigenous inhabitants first encounter though. There had been European trappers and hunters trapping and exploring the entire New England area for scores of years prior to the Pilgrims arrival.

A small monument was erected near the supposed site commemorating the Pilgrim's first encounter somewhere near the beach three hundred years later in 1920. A second plaque was erected in 2001 to better reflect current understandings of the interaction of the two cultures.

The Real First Encounter?

If you want to see the original 1920 monument "location," you will have to do a short bit of walking. From the new plaque at the south end of the parking lot turn around and look towards the other (north) end of the parking lot. You will see a small hill at that end. The location of the original plaque is on the top of that hill. Look for a little path up the hill. It is about fifty feet from the edge of the beach and is not easy to miss. The path is not maintained, so watch out for poison ivy and ticks along the way. You may want to wear long pants. Eventually you will arrive at a small clearing. Congratulations, not a lot of people know about or have seen the original 1920 First Encounter Monument. There is a wrinkle, though. You will only see the rock. The plaque is no longer there because someone pried it off and spirited it away.

Remains of the Original Monument

The inscription on the original plaque reads:

ON THIS SPOT HOSTILE INDIANS HAD THEIR FIRST ENCOUNTER DECEMBER 8 1620 old style WITH MYLES STANDISH JOHN CARVER WILLIAM BRADFORD JOHN TILLEY EDWARD WINSLOW JOHN HOWLAND EDWARD TILLEY RICHARD WARREN STEPHEN HOPKINS EDWARD DOTEY JOHN ALLERTON THOMAS ENGLISH MASTER MATE CLARK MASTER GUNNER COPIN AND THREE SAILORS OF THE MAYFLOWER COMPANY

PROVINCETOWN TERCENTENARY 1620 COMMISSION 1920

The inscription on the newer *parking lot* plaque reads:

NEAR THIS SITE THE NAUSET TRIBE OF THE WAMPANOAG NATION SEEKING TO PROTECT THEMSELVES AND THEIR CULTURE HAD THEIR FIRST ENCOUNTER 8 DECEMBER 1620 WITH MYLES STANDISH, JOHN CARVER, WILLIAM BRADFORD, EDWARD WINSLOW, JOHN TILLEY, EDWARD TILLEY, JOHN HOWLAND, RICHARD WARREN, STEPHEN HOPKINS, EDWARD DOTEY, JOHN ALLERTON, THOMAS ENGLISH, MASTER MATE CLARK, MASTER GUNNER COPIN AND THREE SAILORS OF THE MAYFLOWER COMPANY.

THIS TABLET IS PLACED IN 2001 BY THE SOCIETY OF COLONIAL WARS IN THE COMMONWEALTH OF MASSACHUSETTS

So that is the story about the two "First Encounter Beach" memorials: one in the parking lot and one on the hill overlooking the parking lot. The second location is not difficult to find. You, among your friends, will probably be the only one who will have seen both memorials. If you check Google Maps, though, you will see that they know where the real First Encounter Beach Tercentenary Memorial is located!

To Visit:

Location: The original First Encounter Monument is located at First Encounter Beach on the hill at the north end of the beach parking lot off of Samoset Road. The second First Encounter Monument is located at the south end of the beach parking lot. From Route 6 head west on Samoset Road in Eastham. Follow it to the end. You will drive into the beach parking lot. The popular Monument is at the far (south) end of the parking lot.

If you come during the summer, you will be asked to pay a rather steep beach access fee. If you explain very nicely why you are there, perhaps show the guard this book, and what you want to see the guard may let you pass so you can see the Monument and the stone. If you want to see the original plaque and stone it will take a bit longer to get to (ten minutes) so you might want to arrive early in the morning or latter in the day when the guards are not on duty. Make sure you are well prepared for ticks and poison ivy.

*Bradford, William. (1856). *Of Plimoth plantation 1620-1648.* New York: 'Lil Beethoven Publishing.

10. EASTHAM: CEDAR BANK LINKS: THE GOLF COURSE AND THE GHOST

Historic Sites

Ghosts and Ghouls and Mysterious Shapes

Background

I am sure that one of the first places you sought out when you passed the Orleans rotary was the Cape Cod National Seashore Salt Pond Visitor Center. This Visitor Center is just off Route 6 in Eastham and is located on a low hill on the east side of the highway. There is a long parking lot at the front left of the building. Behind the Visitor Center, the land gently slopes down through woods and paths to the shores of Salt Pond and further to the Nauset Marsh. This little area behind the Visitor Center is a beautiful and peaceful space where many visitors enjoy sitting a bit to relax and take in the view.

View of Salt Pond from the Visitor Center

Many people don't realize the great deal of history stretching back into the early 1800s right here at the location of the present-day Visitor Center. This hill has gone through many usage and physical changes. Over the years, this area has also been associated with several U.S. presidents as well as the ghosts of its past inhabitants.

A History of the Salt Pond

Originally, this area was the home of the Nauset Tribe of the Wampanoag nation, and it was later settled by Europeans in 1644. It is now part of the Town of Eastham, which was incorporated in 1651. In the late 1800s, Eastham was known for great duck hunting, and the premier location for this was Nauset Marsh, the bay shore, and ponds nearby.

This and the solitude of the area attracted many very wealthy Boston families who wanted to escape from the noise, pollution, and bustle of the city. Among the Bostonians who came here were Quincy Adams Shaw, Sr. (1875-1958) and his son Quincy "Quinny" Adams Shaw, Jr. (1897-1987). The Shaws made their money in copper mining in Michigan and were descendants of President John Adams (1797-1801) and President John Adams eldest son, President John Quincy Adams (1825-1829). Since the Shaws wanted to have a home outside of Boston, they found and bought the old Braley Creamery farm which was located south of Nauset Road. Unfortunately, no trace of the Creamery has made it to the present day.

On top of the hill where the Visitor Center is currently located, the Shaws built a hunting lodge: the Cedar Bank Lodge. In 1915, the Harvard-educated mining engineer, Shaw, Sr., suffered a nervous breakdown and was hospitalized in McLean Hospital near Boston for about ten years. When he was finally released, his doctors urged him to find a hobby to occupy his time. After some thought, Shaw, Sr., hired a local farmer named Dan Sparrow, his earth scoop, and his horse, Jerry, and set out to build a golf course on the land near the lodge. Over the next three years, Shaw, Sparrow, and Jerry built an eighteen-hole, par 72, 6,490-yard course. The Boston Evening Transcript described the course as "one of the finest natural layouts in the world." That being said, it was an adventure getting around the course. The course went through and over marshes, tidal pools, and the Salt Pond. I should tell you now that although the positions of the tees and greens are almost the same, *in many cases* there are at least two readily available maps that place tees and greens in quite different locations!

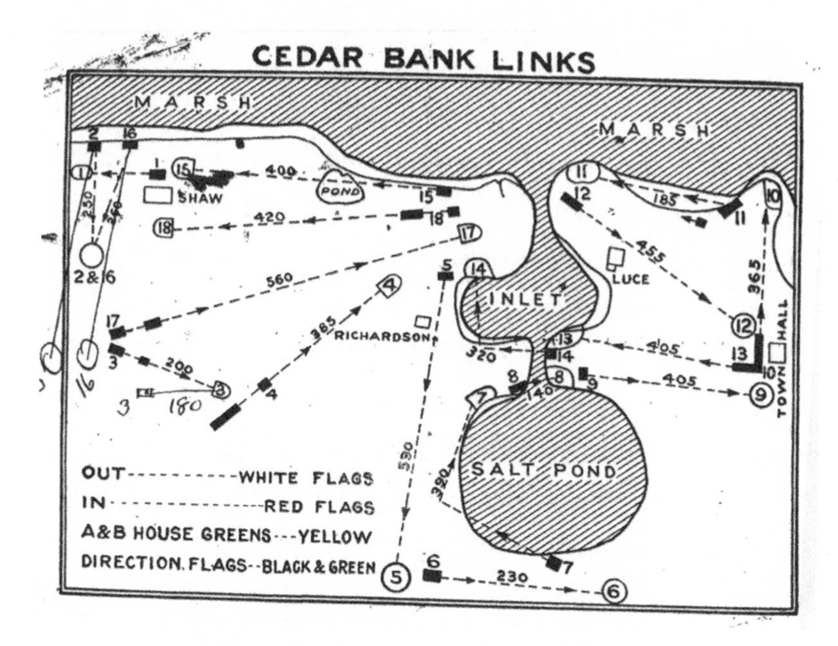

One of the Maps of Cedar Bank Links
(Courtesy of the Eastham Historical Society)

As near as can be determined, the sixth green was located just to the right of the present-day Salt Pond Visitor Center, and the seventh green was between the Visitor Center and Salt Pond. Some other maps suggest that it was the ninth green and it was located near the far end of the parking lot. The twelfth green was located under the current Eastham Town Hall or something like that. (Got all that? You will get a test in the mail.) To get to the eighth green from the eighth tee, players, caddies, and their equipment were loaded onto a barge and the occupants had to use a pulley and rope system to pull everything across Salt Pond inlet! They used the same procedure but in the opposite direction between the fourteenth tee and its corresponding green.

The Golfers

Cedar Links was in use from roughly 1926 until World War II. Such golf luminaries as Bobby Jones and Francis Ouimet played the course. Jones shot a one-over-par 73, the best ever score at Cedar Links; Ouimet managed a 75. Quincy Adams Shaw sold the area to the National Seashore in 1959.

Every Labor Day Quincy Adams Shaw threw a rather unruly but nonetheless exclusive clambake with all the typical Cape Cod fixings from steamers to lobsters. As a tale tells it, one of the former speakers of the Massachusetts House was so upset when he was not invited that he dressed in an at-that-time stereotypical depiction of an indigenous person wearing just a loincloth and "war paint". He then borrowed a canoe and paddled across the pond to crash the party. When the former speaker came into view, he was greeted by a shower of rocks thrown by Shaw and his guests.

Probable Location of the Transit Point

The Cape Cod National Seashore Salt Pond Visitor Center in Eastham has been the sight of several stories involving a ghost who likes to play golf. Many people believe that the ghost that frequents the visitor center is that of Quincy, Sr., endlessly playing golf to help him find peace for his troubled soul.

The Man

A few years ago, I was talking to an old man as we sat together in front of the Provincetown Town Hall. He said that when he was a teen, he saw an old man playing golf on the front lawn of the Salt Pond Visitor Center late one evening. He reported that while he was watching, a fog seemed to overtake the man, and the old man seemed to disappeared into thin air before him.

Over the years, several other people have reported similar experiences. These encounters usually happened on warm, moonlit evenings at about dusk as the people walked or stood near the front of the Visitor Center. Most reports described how the viewer first felt a bone-chilling breeze and soon after heard a loud voice yelling something like, "Put your head down!" "Duck!" or "Get out of the way!" This was typically followed by a sound like someone hitting a golf ball and then something whizzing by their heads.

One older man reported that he did not hear a golf club but instead heard the sound of a gun. Looking back in the direction of the sounds, many say they seemed to have caught a glimpse of a figure of an older man looking in their direction and holding something in his hand. Most of the storytellers have run to their cars at that point. One young couple swore that it looked like the man walked into a tree and disappeared.

To Visit

Location: Cape Cod National Seashore Salt Pond Visitor Center in Eastham on the east side of Route 6 at Nauset Road.

11. EASTHAM: DOANE ROCK, DOANE HOMESTEAD, AND THE SALT (KETTLE) POND STORY

Historic Sites

Overview

Cape Cod has an interesting geological history. With one exception, the Cape is a product of the glaciers that covered northern North America between 18,000 and 25,000 years ago. The exception is the portion of Cape Cod from High Head in North Truro to the tip of the Cape. All of that land is composed of sand carried by the currents on the Atlantic (eastern) side of the Cape northerly and deposited from High Head around to the tip of Long Point in Provincetown. This process is still happening today.

The border line of the maximum advance of the last glacier, known as the Laurentide Ice Sheet, was approximately where the islands of Martha's Vineyard and Nantucket are today. That glacier receded rapidly about 15,500 years ago. The melting ice left rock debris called glacial *drift*. Drift consists of everything from very fine to very coarse sand, gravel, rocks, and stones. Cape Cod is a product of the deposition of that drift. The drift covering or making up Cape Cod is between 200 and 600 feet thick. Drift that is unstratified (a mixture of various sizes) is called *till*.

When a glacier starts to melt, piles of rock and debris are deposited along the melting edge. These are pushed forward by new ice pressing forward from behind. Think of a conveyor belt moving more ice and drift down to the end of the belt. As the ice melts at the end of the conveyor belt, the drift inside will start to pile up. This pile of rock and debris is called a *moraine*. When the edge of the glacier melts it not only deposits a moraine at its leading edge, but the melting glacier also forms streams that carry some of the moraine material away from the melting glacier. This field of debris is called an *outwash plain*. (Got all that? You will get a second test in the mail.) Most of the Cape Cod landscape is an outwash plain.

Sometimes very large chunks of ice were left behind on the moraine or the outwash plain as a glacier receded. As these chunks melted, they formed a depression in the mud or soft sand. The depressions are called *kettles*. On Cape Cod, many of these kettles have filled with fresh water. These ponds, formed by the kettle left by the melting chunk of glacier are called *kettle ponds*. These freshwater kettle ponds have been used as swimming holes for decades (centuries even).

Salt Pond

Salt Pond, behind the Cape Cod National Seashore Salt Pond Visitor Center, is a giant kettle pond. A historical marker near Salt Pond estimates that the ice block covered an area of over four football fields. Salt Pond was originally a fresh water kettle pond. Sometime around 1,200 years ago a channel formed between it and Nauset March. Salt water started to flow in through the channel. Salt Pond's salt content is lower than the ocean because it is fed by fresh water in addition to salt water from the ocean's tidal flow. Surprisingly, even under the changing tidal conditions, it is very rich in both animal and plant life.

Doane Rock

Doane Rock

Just down the road from the Salt Pond Visitor Center is Doane Rock. Doane Rock is the largest exposed glacial rock on Cape Cod. It is eighteen feet high and is thought to extend another twelve feet into the ground. Doane Rock has been resting where it was deposited for between 12,000 and 18,000 years.

Doane Rock was named after John Doane, an early settler. Doane was born in England in about 1590 and first arrived in Plymouth between 1628 and 1632. (Remember the Pilgrims first arrived in Provincetown in 1620.) There is no record of his English ancestry or when or on which boat he arrived in Plymouth. At first it appears that he had some government positions. He resigned his position as Assistant Governor to free himself up for religious duties sometime between 1633 and 1634. During this time, he became one of three deacons of the Plymouth Colony church. Even so, Doane remained active in colonial politics by serving as deputy to the General Court, assistant to the governor and also as a member of the committee that revised the colonial laws in 1636. Deacon Doane was one of the very few individuals who at that time bore the title of "Mr." before his name. Very few early colonists were allowed the privilege of using this title!

Doane Homestead

In 1644, Plymouth Colony (on the mainland) decided to split off the Cape Cod land and set up a second colony with Nawsett (Nauset) being the center. In 1651, the court ordered the town of Nauset to change its name to Eastham. Deacon Doane was assigned to buy the land in Eastham from the Wampanoag tribe for this new colony. He and his family moved to Eastham and were some of the first Europeans to live among the Wampanoags. At that time, the Eastham community consisted of both Wampanoag Indians and European settlers.

In Eastham, Doane was the town deacon of Eastham's first church, a Justice of the Peace, a deputy of the Colony Court, and a member of the first Board of Selectmen. He died at the age of 95 on February 21, 1685, according to the Town Hall plaque, or February 1, 1685, according to his gravestone. He was buried in the Cove Burying Ground in Eastham.

The site of Deacon Doane's former homestead is indicated by a marker several hundred yards down the nearby Doane Trail leading from Doane Rock. The Trail is a paved, wheelchair-accessible .6-mile loop that also passes by the Doane Picnic Area. The house is long gone, but there is a stone outline of its foundation at the site. The homestead is an important archeological site. Doane Rock has been sometimes called Enochs or Enos Rock after the deacon's son. Henry David Thoreau acknowledged Deacon Doane in his book *Cape Cod* written in 1865.

Location of the Doane Homestead

This area contains a great deal of geological and human history, and it's worth spending some time there. In 2019, the University of Michigan even used the area for an archeological field school investigation.

Now you have learned about glaciers, the formation of Cape Cod, kettle ponds, Deacon Doane, the founding of Eastham, Doane Rock, and the location of the Doane homestead! That wasn't so bad…was it?

Recent research seems to indicate that his name was spelled *Done* and that the *Doane* spelling was only used when referring to his children. By the way, there is also a Doane University (established in 1871) in Crete, Nebraska, by Thomas Doane, a descendant of the Deacon, and there is also an active Doane Family Association.

To Visit

Location: 520 Doane Rd, Eastham. From Route 6 in Eastham, go east (toward the ocean) at the Cape Cod National Seashore Salt Pond Visitor Center. You are on Nauset Road. Continue down the road, and when the road splits, continue straight on Doane Road. The distance from Route 6 is about a mile. Take a right on Pinecrest Drive, and the parking area will be on the left. From Doane Rock, take the trail past the bathrooms. Follow it to the site of the Doane homestead. On the way back you can take a short cut through the parking/picnic area. Walk to the far end of the parking lot and continue down the trail on the right a few hundred feet to get to Doane Rock.

The Doane Picnic Area is most easily accessed by continuing on Pinecrest Drive past the Doane Rock parking area. Brown signs will show you the way.

12. WELLFLEET: THE LEGEND OF GOODY HALLETT

Ghosts and Ghouls and Mysterious Shapes

Overview

Everyone likes a good ghost story, and this is one of the best. It involves an attractive young blond (or black haired or brunette or ??) girl known as Goody, her child, and her daring young pirate lover. It has to be a good story line. Even Netflix retold the story of Goody and her lover "Black Sam" Bellamy in a 2021 series titled *The Lost Pirate Kingdom*. Now, let me tell you their sad and spooky tale that has connections to several parts of Cape Cod. I will caution you that for everything I will be telling you, there are probably a score of other versions of the story.

Black Sam

Let's start with Goody's lover. Samuel Bellamy was born in England in 1689. After his service in the British Navy, he found that he liked the sea life and money, and he decided to turn to piracy to earn a living. Though his career as a pirate only lasted a bit over a year, he and his crew managed to capture at least fifty-three ships, and this earned Black Sam the honor of being the wealthiest pirate in recorded history. According to *Forbes* magazine*, he and his crew amassed a fortune worth upwards of $120 million in 2008 dollars. We always hear about "Blackbeard the Pirate," but he was almost destitute being number seven on the pirate's earnings list with only $12.5 million in booty. Number ten on the list (James Martel) only made $1.5 million, and John Ward, the inspiration for Jack Sparrow in *Pirates of the Caribbean*, does not even make the list.

Where Goody Waited for Pirate Sam

Now, back to our story. Bellamy traveled to the Wellfleet area in 1714. According to legend, he met and fell in love with a local teenager—stories say she was fourteen or fifteen years old—by the name of Goody Hallett. Her first name and who she really was has been lost in history. Some legends have her as "Maria" or "Mariah" or "Mehitable," and over five-hundred-sixteen family trees on ancestry.com list her as Mary (Goody) Hallett. Take your pick. This last one (Mary [Goody?] Hallett) was born in

1701 in Eastham and died April 22, 1751, in Yarmouth. As you can see, history and lineage of a legend can be murky. Elizabeth Reynard, in her 1936 book *The Narrow Land*, is said to have made up the name Maria Hallet! Other historians say her name was Mehitable Brown and that she was married when she met Sam Bellamy. And there are stories that Black Sam was also married and had children back home in England. Kathleen Brunelle's book *Bellamy's Bride, The Search for Maria Hallett of Cape Cod* is a great resource for more information.

Anyway, on with the story. Since Goody's parents thought that Sam was too poor and a bad choice for their daughter. Black Sam, wanting to prove himself to Goody and her parents, left Goody and sailed off to seek his fortune. He planned to return and take her away with him.

Goody's Pact

Shortly after Sam left, Goody discovered that she was pregnant. Though not an uncommon occurrence in that day and age, this was considered a major sin against God and society. Because of this, she was ridiculed, bullied, and banished from the community. She ran into the woods near Cedar Swamp Trail at Marconi Beach in Wellfleet and lived alone as an outcast there in an old shack. The child named, some say, Bellamy "Knowles" was born October 1, 1716. Goody hid the baby from the townspeople as best she could. Unfortunately, the child died shortly after birth. Some stories say that the child was stillborn or Goody killed the child, and others say that Goody left the child in some straw in a barn to keep it warm as she went out scavenging for food, and little Bellamy choked on a piece of straw. The townspeople found Goody clutching her dead child, and brought Goody before the local magistrate where she was charged with baby Bellamy's death and arrested for murder. If an unwed mother's child died and there were no witnesses to the death, murder was the automatic charge in New England at the time!

After a public whipping where she begged the people to kill her, Goody was sent to the jail (Old Gaol) in Barnstable (See "Barnstable: The Most Haunted Jail in America" earlier in this book). She was thrown out by her parents and shunned by the townspeople. She was missing her lover, and having lost her child as well as being charged with its murder, and locked in the Barnstable Jail, Goody was depressed and distressed. Some say that she was more beautiful than ever and talked a jailer into releasing her three different times. Each time she was caught and returned. One day, a dapper man came by and offered to get her out of jail. She could not say no, and she signed a pact with him. *A pact with the devil.* Goody "escaped" one night a week later and made it back to her shack in Wellfleet. The authorities had had enough of Goody and decided not to pursue her.

Following her jailbreak, Goody lived in her small shack in the area of Marconi Beach in an area often nicknamed Goody Hallet Meadow (also known as Lucifer Land). The townspeople of Wellfleet thought that Goody was a witch and avoided her. She is still known to this day as "The Witch of Wellfleet."

Entrance to Cedar Swamp Trail

The exact location of her shack is unclear since at that time most of the outer Cape was one big meadow, due to most of the trees having been removed for home and ship building, and firewood. The most educated guess is that the shack was in the fields just south of the White Cedar Swamp Trail at Marconi Beach, though others say that it was in the area where Marconi set up his antennae. Even in the mid twentieth century, children were warned not to go into White Cedar Swamp during twilight or after dark for fear that Goody might appear and take them as her own. Over the years there have also been reports of the sound of a women crying late at night near the entrance to the White Cedar Swamp Trail.

Bedeviled Homecoming

Unfortunately, this was not the end of Goody's suffering. On April 26, 1717, Black Sam returned to Eastham hoping to find her. The devil, wanting Goody for himself, intervened before Black Sam could keep his promise to Goody. A violent nor'easter blew in at midnight. The temperature was frigid, and the winds blew upwards of eighty miles an hour. The visibility was zero. Before Sam could make it to a safe harbor, his ship the *Whydah Gally* was blown onto a sandbar some five hundred feet off the Wellfleet beach, the masts broke just fifteen minutes later and the ship was pushed by the storm into thirty feet of water where she capsized and sank. Black Sam and all but two of his one-hundred-forty-six-man crew were probably lost. One-hundred-and-four bodies were washed ashore, forty-two crew members were unaccounted for, and three known survivors were arrested and sent to the old Barnstable Jail (Old Gaol) before being brought to Boston and hanged. The townspeople were so enraged by what they had seen during the storm that they grabbed pitchforks and torches and chased Goody into White Cedar Swamp where she lived as a lonely hermit until she died (though remember, ancestry.com says she died in Yarmouth).

Some townspeople say that during severe storms you can still see Goody Hallet standing on a bluff in the area of what is now Marconi Beach shaking her raised fist in the storm and yelling a curse into the gale. Many legends have it that Goody recovered some of Sam's treasures and reburied them somewhere in Wellfleet. As it was, most of the $120 million he looted from those fifty-three ships has never been found.

Black Sam Bellamy's ship, the *Whydah*, was discovered off Wellfleet near Marconi Beach in 1982 under five feet of sand in only fourteen feet of water. Artifacts and treasures from it can be seen at the *Whydah* Pirate Museum (674 Route 28, West Yarmouth).

It is said that on dark and moonless nights people have seen Goody Hallet crying as she walks along Marconi Beach desperately searching for poor Sam's body. Several individuals not knowing the legends have gone up to her to ask why she is crying. They have said the air became very cold as they got near her, and before they reach her, she seems to turn, run down the beach and into the water where she disappears beneath the waves. Other witnesses say that at dusk they have seen a young woman crying and carrying a baby while running into the entrance to White Cedar Swamp Trail.

Goody is also said to haunt the old Barnstable Jail and the Jenny Lind Tower. More information on Goody and the Jenny Lind Tower can be found in the chapter "Truro: The Jenny Lind Tower" later in this book.

To Visit

Location: Marconi Beach and the White Cedar Swamp Trail are accessed by taking Marconi Beach Road off of Route 6. The road is on the East (ocean) side and can't be missed, since it is the entrance to Marconi Beach. If you take your first left (Marconi Station Road) and drive to the end you will pass through the now overgrown Goody Hallet Meadow just before you enter the parking lot at the end of the road. The entrance to the White Cedar Swamp Trail is on the left. If you don't take the left onto Marconi Station Road, but instead continue along Marconi Beach Road, you will end up at the Marconi Beach parking lot. Directions to the old Barnstable Jail (The Most Haunted Jail in America) and the Jenny Lind Tower in Truro can be found in these entries elsewhere in this book.

*Forbes Magazine. (2008, Sept 8). Top-Earning Pirates (https://www.forbes.com/2008/09/18/top-earning-pirates-biz-logistics-cx_mw_0919piracy.html?sh=543c071b7263)

13. TRURO (SOUTH): MITRE: 6520TH AIR CONTROL AND WARNING SQUADRON (EXPERIMENTAL) SITE.

Historic Sites

Overview

Because of its out-of-the-way location, Truro has been the location of many visible and invisible activities. The area we will now look at has had both. Some say the area we will talk about was used to develop secret military technology (true) and some say that the Internet was invented there (could very well be). All that remains of this top-secret site are three areas where buildings have been dismantled and several strange cement footings near each. Unfortunately, you missed out on exploring some interesting old buildings because after standing for almost seventy years after they were decommissioned, the last ones were finally removed in late 2023.

From the early 1950s through the early 1990s the United States and Russia were at war. This was not a hot (shooting) war but a so-called cold (words/spies) war. Research into new and better technologies for spying and for stealing technologies were, and still are, the watchwords of the day. Both sides tried to have a competitive advantage when it came to military offense and defense. Early on, the monitoring of planes and the perfection of radar were paramount for a safe co-existence with the Russians. Truro was a town where some of this development took place.

Detecting Soviet Bombers

Many people know or have at least heard about the abandoned Air Force Radar Station located in Truro on Old Dewline Road. But most people have not heard that there is not one but two abandoned Air Force Radar Stations there: one in North Truro and one in South Truro. The one that comes to most of their minds is the one in North Truro. This one is easy to find but unfortunately is now off limits to the general public. We are talking about the one located at the end of Old Dewline Road near the Highland Light. This 110-acre installation was one of twenty-four Air Defense Command radar stations that the Air Force directed the Army Corps of Engineers to construct in 1948. It was placed in service in 1951 and deactivated and turned over to the National Park Service forty-three years later, in 1994. During its tenure as a radar station, it was the home to the 762nd Aircraft Control and Warning Squadron (later renamed the 762nd Radar Squadron). Their job was to detect and warn the military of approaching Russian aircraft. The National Park Service removed what was left of most of the buildings in 2023. Most had been off limits for some time well before 2023 because of disrepair, fear of collapse, and asbestos. It has also been the home of the Payomet Performing Arts Center for a number of years.

Old Dewline Road takes its name from the Dew Line. A line of radar stations across the northern arctic region of Canada stretching from the Aleutian Islands in Alaska, east across Canada to the Farce Islands in Greenland, and finally to Iceland. There were two other lines of radar stations across Canada: the Pinetree Line from Vancouver Island to Newfoundland and the Mid-Canada Line midway between the two. All three were designed to detect Soviet bombers coming over the North Pole to attack Canada and the United States.

Experimenting

During the early years of the cold war there was another large but little-known radar installation in Truro. It was run by Air Force personnel but controlled by a private corporation. Not many people even today know about this base. Hidden deep in the South Truro woods this hush-hush location was once the home of the 6520th Air Control and Warning Squadron (Experimental) run by the super-secret MITRE Corporation (most Air Force documents list the 6520th Experimental as stationed at Hanscom Field, Massachusetts). The 6520th Squadron's base was not a base in the true sense of the word but rather three hidden-away buildings with radar domes and antennae located on top of three widely separated South Truro hills.

6520th Squadron Patch

There was already the large Air Force Radar Station in North Truro at the end of Old Dewline Road, but more needed to be done. The North Truro Radar Station was just that…a radar installation. The South Truro (MITRE) radar station was a bit different. It was an "experimental" station whose task it was to help develop and test new equipment and procedures to optimize radar's full potential.

History

Originally, the country was protected by a volunteer group of civilian plane spotters (Ground Observer Corp) and a loose group of one-hundred-forty-eight radar installations spread across Canada and the United States. The military decided that this was not a very efficient system and wanted a more automated system. The system would later be known as SAGE (Semi-Automatic Ground

Environment) and the military requested that the Massachusetts Institute of Technology (MIT) design it. SAGE was designed to gather information from near and far radar sites, weather information, aircraft flight plans, available missiles and pursuit aircraft, and technical information about hostile aircraft. This information was then stored and processed by computers, and finally specially trained operators would evaluate the findings. The design and perfection of this new radar system was carried out with MIT and Air Force personnel at Hanscom Field, Bedford, Massachusetts. South Truro was one of the locations where the system was tested. The project was so technical and so large that the government formed a not-for-profit corporation called MITRE to coordinate the undertaking.

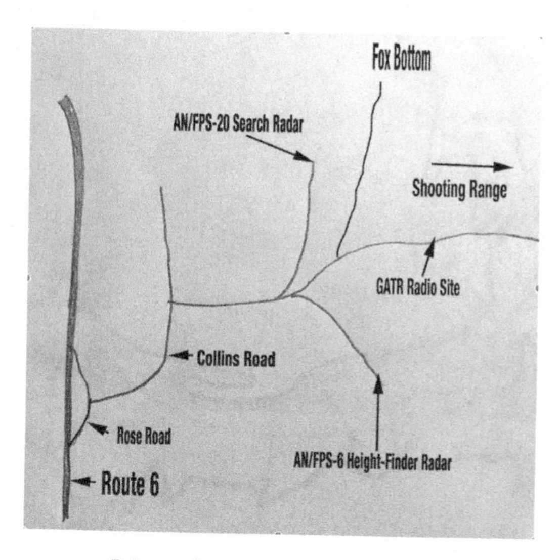

Map of the Truro Radar Site

MITRE Corporation set up three secret experimental radar test sites. MITRE chose the woods of South Truro as one such site. Other sites were in Montauk, Long Island, New York, and West Bath, Maine. MITRE choose the Truro site because of its proximity to the Atlantic and out-of-the way location (it still is). The station was an early part of the SAGE radar network, and the little-known unit, the 6520th Air Control and Warning Squadron (Experimental), manned it. The site was known as ESS (Experimental SAGE Sector), South Truro, Massachusetts. Unfortunately, SAGE was outdated by the time it was up and running. There were two main reasons for this. First, it would be easy for Russian bombers to jam SAGE's radar units, and second, by the time it was deployed, newer intercontinental ballistic missiles made the system too slow to provide any early warning.

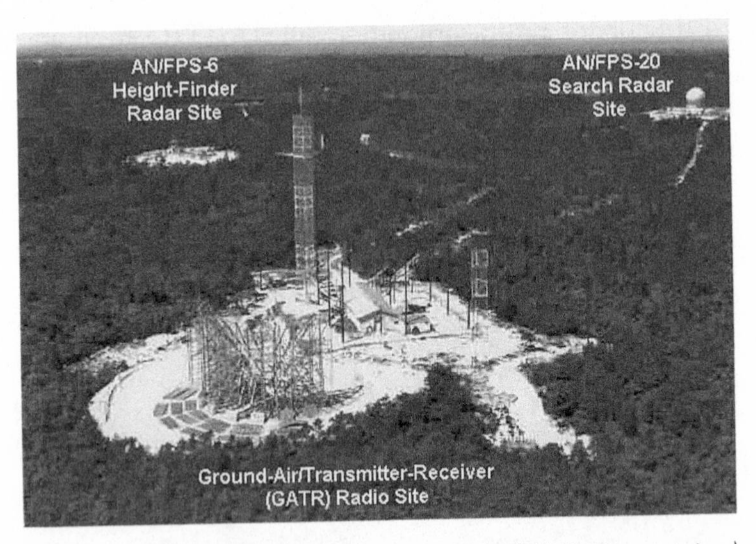

View of the MITRE Site (Courtesy of MITRE Corporation)

All that remained of the site were three cement buildings and cement pads where the AN/FPS-20 (*A*rmy/*N*avy *F*ixed Permanent Land-based Pulsed radar Search *20*th design) Search Radar unit and several antennae were mounted. Since these buildings and antennae were spread out, it appears that this was a large installation. Unfortunately, most of the buildings were removed by the National Park Service in 2023 because they had "no historical significance."

The Internet

Many historians mark the very beginnings of the Internet with the "first" message transmitted from one computer to another by ARPAnet (*A*dvanced *R*esearch *P*rojects *A*gency Network) in the mid 1960s. However, the computers in South Truro were connected and sending data by digital modems to the Whirlwind computer at MIT way back in the 1950s. Some other historians say that perhaps this very simple set-up was an early Internet, and it was first used between South Truro and MIT. (Really, though, the Internet of today uses something called "packet switching technology" which is quite different.)

Ground-Air/Transmitter-Receiver Radio (GATR) Building (Removed in 2023 by the National Park Service)

MITRE is still in existence today and is an interesting "organization." It is not a business as such but rather a "not-for-profit" organization. Forbes (July 13, 2020) described MITRE: *"MITRE Corp. runs some of the U.S. government's most hush-hush science and tech labs. The cloak-and-dagger R&D shop might just be the most important organization you've never heard of."*

BTW: A "mitre" is a tall ceremonial headdress worn by certain Christian bishops and abbots and ancient Jewish high priests. The bishop piece in a chess set is wearing a highly stylized mitre!

To Visit

Location: Fox Bottom Road (abandoned) off Collins Road. From Route 6 just over the town line in South Truro. Go east (Ocean side) onto Rose Road. After a few hundred feet, go east onto Collins Road. Fox Bottom Road is an abandoned road that goes off to the east. It is, or was, paved, and there is a chain across it. It is a popular hiking trail. There is no sign that says what it is. Fox Bottom Road splits into three "roads." The first one goes off to the Search Radar site on the left. The next road off to the right goes to the site of the AN/FPS-6 Height-Finder Radar unit. The next road off to the left will bring you to Fox Bottom Swamp, which, though interesting in itself, has nothing to do with this narrative. The main road will bring you to the GATR (*G*round-*A*ir/*T*ransmitter-*R*eceiver Radio) site. If you continue on down Fox Bottom Road (from this point it is really just a trail) you will pass a shooting range (watch out for shooting practice), and finally you will reach the ocean. It is a nice hike to the ocean and is covered in many trail and hiking websites and books.

13. Truro (South): MITRE: 6520th Air Control and Warning Squadron (Experimental) Site.

14. TRURO: THE CRANBERRY BOG HOUSE

Historic Sites

Overview

Cranberries, cranberries, cranberries…make a little shady depression, fill it with water now and again, keep it damp the rest of the time, wait a long, long time for peat to form, and you will probably have something we call a bog. Peat is an accumulation of plant material, most commonly sphagnum moss, that does not fully decay because the area that it happens to be in is acidic and has little oxygen available (anaerobic). If the bog is in the woods or the dunes in the Cape Cod National Seashore or practically any other location in Massachusetts, you will also probably have cranberries growing there. Cranberries thrive in peaty, acidic soils.

Cranberry plants are low growing (perhaps eight to twelve inches high at most), vine-like plants with small, shiny, oval leaves. Flowers open in May or June and the berries start to ripen in late September or early October.

Cranberries Growing Near the Bog House

Cape Cod is not the only location for cranberries. They can be found growing in the mountains of Georgia all the way north to the Canadian Maritimes. They are found from the Atlantic seaboard west to eastern Minnesota and into the Pacific Northwest. Most people connect cranberries to Massachusetts probably because of the Ocean Spray Cooperative. Do you? Think again...over sixty percent of the U.S. cranberry crop comes from...Wisconsin. Since they are Wisconsin's largest and most profitable crop, I wonder why Wisconsinites wear cheese-head hats and not dark red, round, cranberry-head hats.

Cranberries have been used by indigenous Americans for hundreds of years. The Narragansett Tribe of the Algonquian nation is usually given credit for introducing them to the Pilgrims. The Narragansetts called them *sassamensch*, and Cape Cod's native Wampanoag called them *ibim*; both translate to "sour" or "bitter berries." The indigenous Americans used them for dye and for food, usually by mixing the berries into a concoction called *pemmican*. Pemmican is a mixture of dried meat, tallow, and dried berries if they were available. Tallow is a rendered form of animal fat. I have often wondered why pemmican is not available at the Provincetown Stop & Shop. It is available online though. Interestingly, before McDonald's switched to vegetable oil in 1990, it cooked its French Fries in a mixture of seven percent cottonseed oil and ninety-three percent beef tallow.

The Bogs

You can see cranberry bogs on your way to Cape Cod if you come by way of Route 25 or Route 3. When most people think of cranberry bogs, they usually think of a pond filled with water. Contrary to what you might think (because, again, you have probably seen the Ocean Spray commercial of a father and son in waist deep water harvesting cranberries), cranberries are not aquatic plants. Don't look for them in ponds if you are out cranberrying. During the growing season the bogs are not underwater, though occasionally water may be let in to irrigate the bog. The bogs are flooded at the end of the season to make harvesting easier and also in the winter to protect the plants from freezing temperatures. When the berries are ripe, the bog is flooded, and harvesting machines are driven over the bogs to stir up the water and free the berries from the vines. Ripe berries float to the surface (now remember that ad) and are skimmed off. The best time to harvest berries is after the first frost.

Cranberry Bog House in Truro (Note the location of the Front Door and the Lack of Steps Going Down)

Hiding in the woods in Truro is a remnant of the old-time cranberry industry on Cape Cod. It is called the Bog House. The house was built around 1830 among some cranberry bogs in the Pamet Valley. Around the Bog House are three small bogs along with a system of pipes and drains to control the water levels in the bogs, as previously described. At one time, the bogs were spread over an area of almost ten acres. Now, the little that you see is all that is left of the only commercial cranberry bog operation in Truro.

The Bog House is worth finding. It is a uniquely built and historical building. Also, the front and side doors are on the second floor—and there are no steps down to the ground. This does, of course, create a problem. If you open the front door to step out of the Bog House, you will have one long drop to the ground. You can always leave by the side door. Oh, no you can't. It also is just one long step to the ground! (In the 1880s, the original house was lifted up and a new first floor was added underneath! In doing so they did not bother to remove or change the original entranceways.)

The actual processing of cranberries took place on the bottom floor, and the workers lived on the top floor. The small bogs around the house were in commercial use until the 1960s! In 1998, the National Seashore renovated the house at a cost of $66,000 in federal money, and the Friends of the Cape Cod National Seashore chipped in another $20,000 to help in the restoration.

Please remember that woods = ticks on Cape Cod, and mosquitoes also love bogs, so be prepared. I have been accosted by mosquitoes at the Bog House but never elsewhere on the National Seashore during my fall berry picking.

Path Through the Cranberry Bogs to the Bog House from North Pamet Road

There are two ways to find the Bog House from the parking lot described below. One is to go across the street and take the path through the woods. It is only a short hike and well worth the walk. The other is to walk back down the road to a relatively wide grassy walkway leading through the bogs to the house.

If you decide to collect some cranberries in the National Seashore, you must remember the law: one gallon of cranberries per person per day for personal consumption only.

To Visit

Location: From Route 6 in Truro, go east (ocean side) on North Pamet Road to the end. There is a parking lot next to and to the west of the Youth Hostel and across from the trail head at that location. At this point, you will be at the start of the Pamet Area Trails system. This is not the shortest route to the Bog House. Check your GPS to locate where the Bog House is closest to the road, walk down the road to that location and down a wide path from the road to the house. I would watch out, though. The road can be busy, with many sharp curves, and it is sometimes difficult to see the cars coming down the road and for the drivers to see you.

15. TRURO: CORN HILL

Historic Sites

Overview

The Pilgrims sailed into Provincetown Harbor in November of 1620. It was a horrible sixty-six-day voyage. In their fifty-eight-by-twenty-four-foot damp, icy cold, cramped, smelly, windowless, and dirty living space. Seasickness was rampant. Their limited four-hundred-calorie diet consisted of dried meat, hardtack biscuits, and beer. (The recommended daily calorie intake per day is 2,000 for women and 2,500 for men.)

It is estimated that every man on the voyage lost about twenty-five percent of their body weight. And yet, out of one-hundred-and-two people (forty-one Pilgrims and sixty-one "Strangers") that made the trip, only one died at sea. The *Mayflower* also had a crew of thirty-seven.

Original Corn Hill Monument

Once the *Mayflower* dropped anchor in Provincetown Harbor, the Pilgrims came ashore and did a bit of exploring around the area looking for food and clean water. They then decided to see what lay further to the south. The easiest and quickest way for them to travel down the coast was by boat. Within the confines of the *Mayflower*, the Pilgrims had dismantled and stored a thirty-foot long sailing vessel called a *pinnace* or *shallop*. Unfortunately, it had been damaged during the voyage:

...but being much brused & shatered in ye shipe wth foule weather, they saw she would be longe in mending,

It took about two weeks to repair and reassemble the shallop.

Wherupon a few of them tendered themselves to goe by land and discovere those nearest places, whilst ye shallop was mending...

The shallop was finally repaired, and a party of sixteen men led by Miles Standish, Stephen Hopkins, Edward Tilley, and William Bradford (who wrote the narratives quoted in the text) set out again in search of food. They came ashore at the mouth of the Pamet River in present day Truro and climbed a nearby hill for a better look at the surrounding area. Research and traditions over the years place this hill as the one later given the name Corn Hill.

Corn Hill and the Nauset tribe

As the Pilgrims explored the hill and the surrounding area, they came upon what, from their description, was a recently vacated Nauset people's summer encampment. During the summer the area is pleasant, with nice views and cooling ocean breezes. It would have been an ideal place for such an encampment. During the winter, the area is known for its cold, high winds and would not be a place to live. Around this time, probably late October or early November, the indigenous people would leave this area for more sheltered living and hunting areas in the forest below the hill.

The Pilgrims had timing on their side. It was a good thing that the Nauset people were not in the village. If they were there, history would probably have been much different. The Nauset people had no love for the English. In 1614, Thomas Hunt, an Englishman, abducted twenty Nauset people along with other indigenous people from around New England and sold them into slavery in Spain.

One of the indigenous people was the notable Tisquantum, known to us as Squanto from the Patuxet tribe from along western Cape Cod Bay. Tisquantum was ransomed by some monks and eventually traveled to England where he learned English. He returned to the Cape area in 1619 and helped the Pilgrims and Nausets mend their differences.

The Nauset people probably relocated relatively recently to their winter location since the *"heps of sand newly padled with their hands"* were still visible.

As the party explored the area, they found…

> *a good quantitie of clear ground wher y'e Indeans had formerly set corne… proceedings furder… they fornd wher latly a house had been, wher some planks and a great ketle was remaining and heaps of sand newly padled with their hands, which they, digging up, found in them diverse faire Indean baskets filled with corne, and some in eares, faire and good, of diverse collours, which seemed to them a very goods sight, (haveing never seen any shuch before).*

After some discussion the Pilgrims *"tooke with them parte of y'e corne, buried up y'e rest…"* so they would have some food for the winter and seed to plant the next spring. In all, they took fourteen bushels of corn. They were in dire need of the corn since their provisions from their long ocean voyage were dwindling fast, and taking this corn most likely saved the Pilgrims from starvation. Still, by the spring of 1621, half of the *Mayflower's* original passengers had died from disease, poor food, and bitter cold in the new world. Of course, by this time they had moved on to Plymouth.

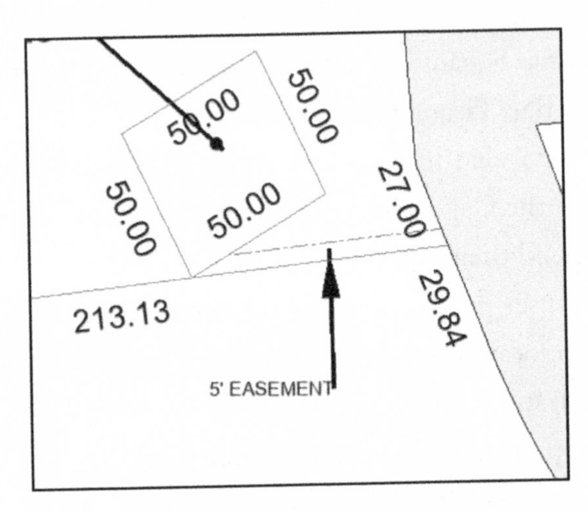

Map Showing the Location of the Original Monument and Easement

The Pilgrims, being religious, were hesitant to take the corn and vowed to pay back the Nauset people. They finally were able to do this about six months later. According to historians, paying back the Nauset people was also a great diplomatic move, as it helped secure the trust and peace with the Nauset people for the next fifty years. All of this happened in the Corn Hill region of Truro.

There are two monuments marking this event. The original monument was constructed to mark the "location" of the cache of corn on the hill that is now called Corn Hill. This monument is about a foot high by fourteen inches wide by six inches thick. The inscription reads simply: "CORNHILL 1620." Very few people know about this marker or where it is located. This (original) monument's location is near the top of Corn Hill at the end of an overgrown path about seventy-five feet up the right side of a bayside driveway to a cottage compound at 62 Corn Hill Road. This is a private driveway. The marker is in the center of a fifty-by-fifty-foot plot legally accessed by a five-foot-wide easement to the right of the driveway and on the left edge of the next property at 64 Corn Hill Road. A newer monument was constructed in 1920 by the Provincetown Tercentenary Commission at the north end of the Corn Hill Beach parking lot. This plaque is easily accessible.

New Corn Hill Monument (Left) at the Beach Parking Lot

To Visit

Location: 39 Corn Hill Rd., Truro. From Route 6, take Castle Road .7 miles on the west (Bay) side. Turn right on Corn Hill Road for .7 miles, and the Monument is on the left by the flagpole at the north end of Corn Hill Beach parking lot. (Access may be limited during the day in the summer as this is a Truro beach parking lot. Check with parking attendant.)

16. TRURO (NORTH): THE JENNY LIND TOWER

Historic Sites

Ghosts and Ghouls and Mysterious Shapes

Overview

Many visitors who come to Cape Cod are interested in history, want to see lighthouses, get in some beach time, just relax, and/or want to play a little golf. One area that has at least three of the four activities within feet of each other is the Highland area of North Truro. After turning off South Highland Road onto Highland Light Road, you will immediately see a parking area on your right, Highland Light (previously called Cape Cod Light) straight ahead, the Highland House Museum to your left, and between the Highland House Museum and the Highland Light, you will see the Highland Links golf course. For many years, North Truro was considered the center of Truro, and because of this, the Highland area of North Truro still holds a number of locations and buildings that have contributed to the history, folklore, and life of not only Truro but the whole of Cape Cod. If you read the section on Marconi found elsewhere in this book, you may remember that the Highland area was the site where Marconi originally wanted buy the land to build his wireless station. However, the townspeople, thinking he was a fraud and a quack, turned him down. He eventually built his station in Wellfleet, but because of winds and erosion, he later moved it to Chatham.

The Highland House and Light

The Highland House Museum is the home of the Truro Historical Society, which in itself is worth a look. Not only are the displays and artifacts interesting, but the building is of historical significance. It was built in 1907 as a seasonal hotel called *The Highland House.* For well over one-hundred-fifty years, tourists have been coming to Cape Cod to escape the summer heat in the New England cities and New York. Even if you are saying, "Been there, done that," you may want to check out the museum again because they change their exhibits often.

Partially surrounding the museum and the Highland Light, and almost all the way back around to the parking lot on the right is Highland Links. Highland Links is one of Cape Cod's oldest golf courses (1892), described by Alistair Cook, a British journalist and radio and television personality in the late twentieth century, as "the most perfect example of the typical British or Scottish links in the United States."

View of the Jenny Lind Tower from Highland Golf Course

While in the area, you should walk up to Highland Light, the oldest and tallest lighthouse on Cape Cod. The current tower was built in 1857, replacing lights built in 1797 and 1831. It was originally commissioned by George Washington and is still actively used today. Because of coastal erosion, Highland Light was moved back to its present position in the mid-1990s. You can climb up to the top during the summer...you can even get a special permit to climb to the top and get married!

Who is Jenny Lind?

There is another unusual piece of history and lore present out here on the bluffs. Just to the southeast of the Highland area (to your right as you walk towards the ocean) and nestled in the woods is a round stone tower jutting out from the landscape. It kind of looks like something out of a King Arthur movie. It is not uncommon to see people gawking at it, photographing it, and asking about this strange tower.

This medieval look-alike is named the Jenny Lind Tower. The story of this tower and how it arrived at its current location has many variations. One can say with confidence (probably the only parts of the story you can say this about) is that it is named after the nineteenth-century opera singer named Jenny Lind, also known as "The Swedish Nightingale." We also know that the tower was once part of the Fitchburg (Massachusetts) Railroad depot built in 1842 on Causeway Street in Boston. That route is now part of the Purple Commuter line to Boston. Ok, there are three things you can be sure of.

As you read the following, you must remember that P.T. Barnum (*"There is a sucker born every minute!"*) was the promoter of Ms. Lind's tour. He paid her the unbelievable sum of just under $25 million in today's dollars for her nine months in the United States. But then again, at her concerts you could buy everything from Jenny Lind paper dolls to Jenny Lind branded chewing tobacco!

Jenny Lind Tower

One of the often-told stories linking this tower to Ms. Lind, be it myth, embellishment, or truth, concerns a concert she gave in Fitchburg, Massachusetts. On the 14th of October 1850, Jenny Lind gave an oversold (as Barnum often did) concert in the auditorium at the Fitchburg Railroad depot. As the story goes, she had to cut her performance short because the ticket-holders who were not allowed to enter because the depot had reached capacity crashed through the gates, breaking doors and windows and causing mischief and mayhem. Numerous stories abound about what happened next, but the most popular legend goes that Ms. Lind climbed to the top of (that very) tower and sang to the crowd below. Another story says that *after* her encore, she went up to the top of the tower to give another encore to the throngs waiting to hear her outside the venue. Either way, there was nothing in any of the local papers about what may or may not have happened.

The depot was torn down in 1927, and a Boston lawyer by the name of Henry M. Aldrich had one tower dismantled and moved to North Truro where he owned a piece of land. Mr. Aldrich paid five men to reassemble the massive cut granite blocks of the tower and to also build five cottages nearby. Other legends regarding why he moved that tower say that Mr. Aldrich was captivated by Jenny Lind's voice, even though she sang seventeen years before he was born or that a family member who loved her voice begged him to move the tower to their land in Truro or that he moved the tower because he loved trains. One of Aldrich's sons later said that Lind had nothing to do with his father's reasons to move the tower to Truro! Sadly, we will never know the real story.

We can say, though, that the Jenny Lind Tower is seventy-two feet high (about five or six stories) and fifteen feet in diameter at its base. It is in the middle of a harsh thicket of brambles, poison ivy, ticks, and other assorted hazards several hundred feet east of the FAA radar dome (which you can also see when you look at the tower). From the southern side, it is located just north of the now abandoned North Truro Air Force Station at the end of Old Dewline Road.

View Looking Up the Inside of the Jenny Lind Tower

One chapter in this book describes Goody Hallett, the "Witch of Wellfleet," and how her lover, the famed pirate "Black" Sam Bellamy, disappeared in the waters off Wellfleet when his ship the *Whydah Gally* went down in a storm in 1717. Goody has been haunting the woods from Eastham to Truro ever since. According to legend, Goody lets out a banshee-like cry as she begins her hauntings. Sailors' tales tell of how just her cry has caused ships to sink. When Goody's cry starts, the ghost of Jenny Lind is said to climb to the top of the tower and begin to sing. Her beautiful nightingale-like voice is said to repel Goody and frighten her away from the Truro woods. People in the area will tell you that this is not the whole story. Ms. Lind can also be heard singing her songs from the tower on clear, warm spring and summer nights. So, if you are in the area and hear her singing, you are in the clear either way.

To Visit

Location: The tower is not something the National Seashore wants you to visit. Go to the end of Old Dewline Road in North Truro. There was a sign at the road that goes off to the left at the end of Old Dewline that stated, "NO TRESPASSING." You will be on Government property. Otherwise, if you do venture down the road, you will come to a gate at the end of the road, follow the fence to the left. Go around the first corner of the fence, and when you reach the second corner you will see a path into the woods on your left. The tower is about fifty feet down this path through poison ivy and ticks. Trust me, though: it is a Plymouth Rock experience, you will be less than impressed. Once you get to the tower, you will just say: "Oh". You can walk around the tower and look inside, but you can't climb it. All the interior wooden framing and stairs were removed long ago. It is now just a hollow shell. The area can be very dangerous, so do you really want to mess with the FAA, Uncle Sam, and ticks?

17. TRURO (NORTH): UFOS AND THE POND VILLAGE ABDUCTION

Legends and Lore

Overview

To be honest, I did not know what category to put this under. As time progresses this may be labeled "History" or left here as "Legends and Lore." I guess you will have to decide for yourself which label it should have.

Anyone familiar with the lower Cape knows that over the years there have been numerous reports of UFO sightings in the area. One of the more famous ones was the one told by artist (Museum of Fine Arts in Boston, the Guggenheim, The Metropolitan Museum of Art, and the Museum of Modern Art in New York, to name just a few), author, and later ufologist Budd Hopkins, describing his own UFO sighting in August of 1964. Hopkins, his wife, and a friend were traveling from Truro to Provincetown to attend a cocktail party when they encountered a giant metallic, elliptically shaped object hovering soundlessly above the dunes near East Harbor (formerly called Pilgrim Lake) on Route 6. They stopped the car and observed the object for several minutes until it moved behind some clouds and disappeared. At the time, Hopkins thought that it might be some sort of unmanned alien probe. When talking with other friends about the incident, he found that several of them had similar stories to tell. Just like Mr. Hopkins's story, their stories also involved happenings in the Provincetown/North Truro area.

Another Encounter

Another UFO sighting, or perhaps we should say encounter, was reported by columnist and astrologer Carolyn Miller. One warm summer night in the early 1970s, Ms. Miller and her dog took a walk to her family's secluded family home deep in the woods of the National Seashore in North Truro. There she planned to spend the night. She was awakened around midnight by a loud static sound. She thought that it might be park rangers talking on their walkie talkies. She remembers looking at her dog who was staring out the glass sliding door. His hair appeared to be standing straight up on end. A bright light appeared in the window as the noise grew louder. The next thing she remembers is she was standing outside looking at the sun coming up through the trees.

Salty Market Farmstand (Former Dutra's Market)

In an article in the *Provincetown Magazine* several years ago, Ms. Miller was quoted as saying:

"Most everyone who has lived on Pond Road has reported seeing really strange things...Just recently someone saw lights hovering over the old church there."

The article also mentions that "...the area (Pond Village) near North Truro village... appears to be the epicenter of alien visitations."

Yikes, that is just a 10-minute walk from my house.

The Airman and the UFO

Another famous encounter took place adjacent to Pond Village during the time that North Truro was the location of an Air Force Radar Station. This was the 762nd Aircraft Control and Warning Squadron, which was active in North Truro from December of 1950 up until 1985. The Squadron went through several name changes and at the end was known as the 762nd Radar Squadron. This story involves an airman from the base.

It all started at 20:45 (8:45 pm) October 1, 1966. At that time, Airman First Class Robert Matthews stepped off the bus in front of an old nineteenth-century home later repurposed as a general store called Dutra's Market (now called Salty Market Farmstand) at the intersection of Route 6A and Highland Road. The area of North Truro known as Pond Village starts just east of that intersection. This was the first assignment for the nineteen-year-old recent inductee into the Air Force. Truro was a dark and lonely area back in the '60s and it sure wasn't like Airman Matthews bustling hometown of Philadelphia. He had arrived at this dark and lonely spot seemingly in the middle of nowhere and was told to go to the nearby pay phone outside the market and call the North Truro Air Force Station for a ride to the base.

After he made the call some strange things started to happen. At first, he saw bright lights moving back and forth in the sky above him. Within a few minutes, the bright lights approached him. His immediate thought was that the lights were from an Air Force jeep coming to pick him up. However, as the lights became clearer, he saw that they were not coming along the road, but instead there were three bright lights coming towards him a little above tree top level.

This really frightened young Matthews who immediately went back to the phone and called the base for a second time. The person at the other end asked him where he was. Matthews said that he was still at Dutra's Market waiting for a ride. The person at the other end said the base had sent a truck down to pick him up five minutes after he called and the driver could not find him! It was now 21:45 (9:45 pm). The person from the Air Force base wanted to know where he had been for the past hour? Matthews swore that it had only been about four minutes between calls.

Abandoned North Truro Radar Station on Old Dewline Road

When Matthews finally arrived at the base, two men in *civilian clothes* questioned him about what had happened. Matthews was unable to recall any other details for them. What exactly happened on that night at that lonely intersection was still a mystery.

Fast-forward to 1987: Matthews came across a book by Budd Hopkins (remember him?) discussing his research into the "missing time" phenomenon that some people say they experienced when they encountered UFOs. It was the cover of the book, though, that caught Matthew's eye and it gave him a chill. The picture on the cover of Hopkins book was remarkably similar to an experience he had as a child. When Matthews was about six years old, a glowing green figure appeared in his bedroom. He tried to scream, but nothing came out. The figure approached him, lifted him up, and did something to his chest. As you might suspect, when he told his parents what happened that night, they did not believe him.

Matthews contacted Hopkins and told him his story. Hopkins said that he was in Truro in 1964 and relayed his UFO sighting. Hopkins urged Matthews to undergo hypnosis to see what he could recall, if anything.

As a result of hypnosis, Matthews remembered more details. He said that as he waited to be picked up to go to the Air Force base, one of the lights, a red one, flew over near him and enlarged into a space craft. Through a door in the craft, he saw what looked like a doctor's office. At that point, a ramp extended towards where he was standing and he walked up into the craft. The next thing he remembered was that he was very cold and several "beings" started probing him, examining his chest, and taking blood and skin samples.

Matthew's story was featured in season one* (1988) and retold in season five (1995) of the television series *Unsolved Mysteries*.

There are several other UFO sightings and stories from this area of North Truro from the '60s right up through the present day. What do you think? Worth an evening out? I would stay in the car. There are lots of mosquitoes in the area. They will also probe you and take your blood.

To Visit

Location: From Route 6 in North Truro, take the Highland Road, Highland Light exit. Drive towards the bay (west). Go about a tenth of a mile to the corner of Highland Road and Route 6A. Salty Market Farmstand is on the right. At one time a previous owner sold t-shirts with a drawing of the Market with a UFO hovering above. The North Truro Air Force Station is now the home of the Payomet Performing Arts Center, and unless there is a show, it is closed to the public.

**Unsolved Mysteries* Season One, Episode 10 is available on YouTube: (https://www.youtube.com/watch?v=AetYIQEIKYw).

18. TRURO (NORTH): HIGHLAND LIFE-SAVING STATION

Historic Sites

Overview

The shifting sands under the waters around Cape Cod are filled with the wreckage of as many as 3,000 ships along the forty-mile stretch of coast from Provincetown to Chatham. So many ships have gone down and so many people have lost their lives along this coast that many historians call the area off Cape Cod "The Graveyard of the Atlantic." At any given time, the bones of at least one of these ships can be seen popping out of the sand along one of its beaches. Ask at one of the National Seashore Visitor Centers if any have been sighted recently.

Shipwrecks and Shacks

Prior to the establishment of the Life-Saving Service, getting to shore safely from a stranded ship was a hit-or-miss proposition. Numerous attempts were made to help individuals who were fortunate enough to make it to dry land. Unfortunately, most of the ships that ran aground on one of the many shifting sandbars all along the coast usually occurred during one of the horrible winter storms. Often, the winds and water from these storms would pound against the ship causing it to break apart and dooming the crew and any passengers unlucky enough to be caught in it.

Remains of the Bark Francis (1872) at Head of the Meadow Beach

During the early 1800s, there were at least two shipwrecks along the coast every month during the winter. Getting to shore was not easy, and those few who made it were tired, wet, and cold and usually found themselves on a desolate stretch of beach. Many of the "lucky ones" who got to shore simply froze to death in the wind and the cold when they got there. Several towns erected small shacks along the sea's edge with wood and dry clothes or blankets in them to hopefully help the stranded sailors until help arrived. Unfortunately, most of these shacks were looked after by volunteers on a rudimentary basis and were often in disrepair and empty of provisions.

Because of the high number of seemingly needless deaths from shipwrecks, a group of prominent Bostonians formed the

Humane Society of the Commonwealth of Massachusetts. It was patterned after the Royal Humane Society formed twelve years earlier in Great Britain. In 1786, the Massachusetts Humane Society started placing shelters containing food and equipment along the coast of Massachusetts to aid shipwrecked sailors who were fortunate enough to make it to shore. The Society started teaching rescue skills and eventually built and outfitted fifty shacks along the Massachusetts coast.

USLSS

It was not until 1848 that the U.S. Congress approved and funded the formation of the United States Life-Saving Service (USLSS) under the Treasury Department and loosely patterned after the Massachusetts Humane Society. The motto of the USLSS was, "You have to go out, but you don't have to come back." The USLSS was not established on Cape Cod until the 1870s. On Cape Cod, their members were commonly said to be "Guardians of the Ocean Graveyard."

The Highland Life-Saving Station was built in 1872, part of the first nine stations built on Cape Cod. It was located near Coast Guard Beach just north of Highland Light in North Truro. The other eight stations were built at Race Point, Peaked Hill Bars, Pamet, Cahoon's Hollow, Nauset, Orleans, Chatham, and Monomoy Point. Each station was manned by six or seven surfmen and a supervisor or keeper. They watched for ships and sailors in distress 24/7 for ten months a year. All night long men from each station patrolled half way to the next station, met the surfman from the next station, exchanged a small medallion, and walked back home again. Highland Life-Saving Station was officially known as "USLSS Station #8, Second District Coast Guard Station #36."

In 1888, eighteen years after it was first built, "extensive repairs and improvements" were completed at the station.

Highland Life-Saving Station (1891) (Public Domain)

At the time the USLSS was formed, there was a second service designed to interact with ships at sea. This was the Revenue Cutter Service, also part of the Treasury Department, and formed to stop smugglers and enforce trade laws and federal tariffs at sea. It was established by an act of Congress on August 4, 1790, upon the recommendation of Alexander Hamilton who was Secretary of the Treasury. The Revenue Cutter Service and the USLSS were merged on January 28, 1915, by an act signed by President Woodrow Wilson to form the United States Coast Guard. Few people realize that the Coast Guard is one of the six branches of the United States military.

During World War II, the Highland station was manned by eight men, and major equipment located at the station included two pulling boats, an amphibious truck (a DUKW or duck, in common parlance, like they tour people around in Boston), a beach apparatus service cart and two miscellaneous trucks. In April of 1947, the Highland station was merged with the Cape Cod Light Station (Cape Cod Light is now known as Highland Light) and renamed the Cape Cod Light and Lifeboat Station.

The last known records from the station were from mid-1952. The General Services Administration (GSA) (which constructs and manages federal property, auctions, leasing and surplus properties) took the Lifeboat Station over in 1955, and the National Park Service acquired the property in 1969.

Trailhead at Coast Guard Beach Parking Lot to the Highland Life-Saving Station Site

Seeing the Station

The station buildings were torn down in 1958, but you can still see the remains of them on a bluff overlooking Coast Guard Beach in

North Truro. Here, parts of the paved parking area and structural remains are still visible. It is a bit of a climb to find the remains, but the view from the station's location is exceptional.

If you want to see an original Life-Saving Station, Old Harbor Life-Saving Station built in 1897 in Chatham and moved to Race Point Beach in Provincetown in 1977 is now open as a free museum. Read the description of Old Harbor LSS elsewhere in this book. The National Park Service stages life-saving drills, complete with cannon (Lyle gun), for free at Old Harbor on Thursdays during the summer.

Partial Remains of the Highland Life-Saving Station

There are two other original life-saving stations along the Cape Cod coast, though only one is accessible to the public. One is located at Cahoon Hollow Beach in Wellfleet. It is the *Beachcomber*, a restaurant/bar/night club that serves food and drink (it is still a lifesaver after a tired and hot day on the beach). Don't be surprised if you have to wait in line an hour or two during the summer just to get in. There is a third surviving station which is now a private home.

To Visit

Location: The remains of the Highland Life Saving Station are three-quarters of a mile northwest of Cape Cod (Highland) Light. Take the Highland Road, Cape Cod Light exit off of Route 6 in North Truro. Travel east (towards the ocean) until you come to a "T" where Highland Road takes a sharp turn to the right. Don't do this; instead, take the sharp left onto Coast Guard Road. Follow this to the parking lot at the end. There are only ten parking spaces, and you will need a Truro Beach sticker to park there in the summer. On the left-hand side of the parking lot there is a path to the beach. About twenty feet down the path from the parking lot there is a path going off to the left heading up to the top of the dune. Take this path up to the top.

19. TRURO AND PROVINCETOWN: A REAL-LIFE HORROR STORY: TONY COSTA

Historic Sites

Ghosts and Ghouls and Mysterious Shapes

Overview

Nestled deep in the woods of the Cape Cod National Seashore, off of Old County Road in South Truro, and located at the end of a little traveled road called (appropriately) Cemetery Road, you will find the Pine Grove Cemetery. It is a bit off the beaten path but not at all difficult to find. It is a peaceful spot and would be a serene place to rest your weary bones. Unfortunately, all of the accommodations are spoken for. Pine Grove Cemetery, established in 1799, is the second oldest cemetery in Truro. It was originally located next to a Methodist Meeting House. Unfortunately, this building has not survived the passage of time. At one time, the Meeting House and cemetery were located in the middle of an open field, but now they are surrounded by a thick wood. Of the eight-hundred-plus gravestones, the oldest is for James Paine, who died on December, 11, 1799 at the age of fifty-nine. Interestingly, the oldest memorial marker is of one Reuben Rich, a twenty-three-year-old who died in Charleston, South Carolina, in 1796. The most recent stone I found was from 2015, though I have been told that there are several newer ones. This very peaceful but out of the way location served as a focal point for one of the most infamous serial murderers on Cape Cod.

The Murders

The story started to unfold on February 7, 1969, when the body of a troubled local teen, Susan Perry (age seventeen), who had been missing since September 8, 1968, was found at Pine Grove Cemetery. She had been cut into eight pieces.

Pine Grove Cemetery Receiving Tomb

Since there were other recent disappearances of young women in the Provincetown area, police continued digging in the surrounding woods. On March 4, 1969, the head and torso of Mary Anne Wysocki (twenty-three), an education major at Rhode Island College, and the bodies of a second-grade teacher,

Patricia Walsh, (also twenty-three), both last seen on February 4, 1969, and a local waitress, Sydney Lee Monzon, (eighteen) missing since Memorial Day of 1968 were also found near the cemetery. Both Ms. Wysocki and Ms. Monzon had been shot. Further investigations found that they had been dismembered in a similar manner in the old brick crypt (the Receiving Tomb) in the cemetery. The body parts were then moved to a patch of cannabis growing nearby. Several of the body parts had bite marks on them. From that point on the media labeled the killer "The Cape Cod Vampire."

Susan Perry was the girlfriend of a young local carpenter, Anthone 'Tony' Costa (twenty-four). Tony was divorced and the father of three children. The police suspected him for her murder right away. When Patricia Walsh and Mary Ann Wysocki went missing and Susan Perry's body was found, Costa became a person of interest. Walsh and Wysocki had rented a room in the same guest house as Costa at 5 Standish Street in Provincetown. The landlady had introduced them to Tony, and they became fast friends.

5 Standish Street

Further investigation revealed to police that Walsh's and Wysocki's Volkswagen was seen in the woods in Truro on February 2, 1969, a few days before they disappeared. Shortly after it was seen, Costa had asked a local repair shop how much it would cost to have a Volkswagen repainted. Five days later, on February 7, the police returned to the same area and found a piece of fabric sticking out of some newly worked ground. It was from clothing from the cut-up body of Susan Perry. In the meantime, Costa had driven Walsh's car to Boston and Burlington, Vermont. Police found the car in a storage area paid for by Costa in Burlington. When Costa heard that he was under suspicion, he returned to Provincetown to profess his innocence.

Again on March 5, police searched the area where Perry was found and discovered the mutilated bodies of Wysocki and Walsh and the partially decomposed body later identified as Monzon.

All of these were found in the place that Costa called his "Secret Garden," a favorite spot where Costa would take young women to do drugs. When the police learned of the connection between Costa and the garden, they arrested Costa. Since Costa and his family once lived at a guest house at 11 Hughes Road in Truro, the police decided to dig up the cesspool in the hopes of finding any clues or other body parts that may have ended up in there. However, they did not find anything.

11 Hughes Road

Chop Chop

Best-selling author and playwright Kurt Vonnegut's *(Slaughterhouse-five, Cat's Cradle, Happy Birthday, Wanda June)* daughter, Edith (nineteen) became friends with Costa one summer and was even invited to the cannabis garden behind Pine Grove Cemetery with him. Luckily, she declined.

Most people found Costa to be a nice, likeable guy. Ms. Vonnegut found it hard to believe that Costa could be a murderer. He was Liz Rodman's babysitter on and off for a few summers. In her book about Costa, she described him this way: "He seemed to really like being with us. He never yelled. He was really gentle." Several other people though who knew Costa said that he showed sadistic tendencies early in life.

Antone Charles (Tony) Costa was born in Cambridge, Massachusetts, on August 2, 1944, to Antone Fonesca and Cecelia (Bent) Costa. Tony never knew his dad who died eight months after he was born (April 21, 1945) during World War II.

Costa (now known as "Tony Chop Chop" in the media) was tried for the murder of the three women (Wysocki, Walsh, and Monzon), though he is suspected in as many as eight other murders. These crimes included a woman he once lived with in San Francisco, two other young women he once drove to Pennsylvania who had all disappeared, and a woman he dated who was found under suspicious circumstances drowned in her bathtub. He was convicted of the murders of Wysocki and Walsh and sentenced to life in prison on May 29, 1969. Several sources say that when asked in court if there was anything he would like to say, he reportedly replied, "Keep digging."

Costa's mother remarried and later died at the age of sixty-one of a cerebral hemorrhage, eight months after her son was sentenced on December 21, 1969. Costa committed suicide by hanging in Walpole prison on May 12, 1974, at the age of twenty-nine, though many believe that he was killed by other inmates. He is buried in an unmarked grave next to his mother in St. Peter the Apostle Cemetery in Provincetown.

I purposely did not go into many of the grisly details here. You can read more information in Leo Damore's book *In His Garden* from 1981, John Haters 2019 book *Mr. Know-It-All*, Liz Rodmans's 2021 book *The Babysitter: My Summers With a Serial Killer*, the documentary *Twisted: "The Cape Cod Casanova,"* numerous websites, and in *BrnToKil, S6E5 Tony Costa* on YouTube.

Ghosts and Ghouls and Mysterious Shapes

Pine Grove Cemetery is a beautiful and serene place, but knowing the story, Pine Grove is not a place you may want to go to alone, and you definitely don't want to go there in the evening or at night. At least four young women were violently killed and dismembered there, and in Costa's own words in court: "Keep digging." Several reports of spirits, apparitions, and ghosts have been reported there over the years, along with eerie sounds and cries. Cold winds and breezes have been felt as if out of nowhere on hot days, and the woods behind the cemetery where the "secret garden" was located can be eerily quiet. The crypt where the bodies of the women were dismembered was also used to store other bodies when the ground was too hard to dig into. It is still at the far end of the cemetery. This was a real crime scene.

In 2007, the New England Society of Paranormal Investigators investigated the cemetery and surrounding wooded area. They documented cold spots actually moving around the rear of the cemetery. At these locations, their microphones and camera batteries went dead (poor choice of words…). The crew reported that they asked questions and received "answers" from several of the ghosts using special equipment and K2 meters through a process known as EVP (Electronic Voice Phenomena).

The "garden" was near a crossroad at the back of the cemetery. As quoted in *Life* Magazine of July 25, 1969, Evelyn Lawson wrote in the *Provincetown Register*: *"As Dinis (the district attorney) talked…I felt my skin prickle in dread and disgust. The place where the bodies had been found… was near an old cemetery, not far from a back dirt crossroad, the typical traditional site for the witches' Sabbath…"*

To Visit

Location: Old Cemetery Road off of Old Country Road, Truro. Traveling on Route 6, take the Truro Center exit. If you are coming from the north, take your first left onto Depot Road. If coming from the south, take a right at the end of the exit and a right onto South Pamet Road. Go under Route 6 and take a left at the stop sign. Take your first right onto Depot Road. After about .5 miles on Depot Road go right onto Old County Road. Follow Old County Road about 1.1 miles and turn left onto Cemetery

Road. Pine Grove Cemetery is at the end of the road (.4 miles). The brick crypt (Receiving Tomb) is located to the left rear of the cemetery.

The guest houses are at 5 Standish Street in Provincetown and 11 Hughes Road in North Truro and are privately owned. All of this happened almost sixty years ago when these buildings were owned by other individuals. Please don't disturb or bother the owners or any tenants.

Antone "Tony" Costa is buried in an unmarked grave next to his mother Celia Bent Bonaviri under a tree in St. Peter the Apostle Cemetery across from 40 Winslow Street in Provincetown.

20. PROVINCETOWN: OLD MARY OF BEECH FOREST

Historic Sites

Overview

The one thing that always amazes me here on the lower cape is the people. It is not unusual to find that a friend, an acquaintance, someone you just happen to talk to at the grocery store, or even your neighbor—just a regular person—is really a famous, powerful, or well-connected individual, celebrity or government official. Many of them use the Outer Cape as a place to escape from prying eyes and notoriety. They want to be out of the spotlight. Other people just like the peace and serenity of this beautiful area. It is so easy to be just ten minutes from fun-loving Provincetown and yet lost in nature. If you are walking down the street and see someone "who looks a bit like..." it probably is. I could list...but I won't.

One such personage was Mary Oliver. To many in Provincetown, she was a good friend, a neighbor, or just that old lady down the street. To others, she was a little bit difficult. (I guess we all can be at times.) However, to the world at large, she was thought of much differently. Mary was a nationally recognized and, dare we say, world-famous poet. Being a famous poet, she had a long string of honors and awards.

The Poet

Mary's early poetry was mostly about her native Ohio. For personal reasons, in the early 1960s at the age of twenty-eight, she moved to Provincetown, and this wonderful area became the inspiration for most of her later poetry. The poetry she wrote in Provincetown described nature, animals, plants, and communing with nature.

Even though famous, she was a very private person and enjoyed the peace and solitude of living in Provincetown, which was also reflected in her later poetry. Here she lived with the love of her life, photographer Molly Malone Cook, at 535 Commercial Street just west (to the right) of Fanizzi's Restaurant.

Beech Forest Trailhead at the Parking Lot

She first met Cook at the home of Edna St. Vincent Millay in Austerlitz, New York, in 1958. Cook and Oliver were together until Cook's death at age eighty in 2005. Mary lived at 535 Commercial Street from 1964 to 2014. She died of lymphoma on January 17, 2019, in Hobe Sound, Florida, at the age of eighty-three.

Mary Oliver's fifth collection of poems (for *American Primitive*) won the Pulitzer Prize in 1984. She also won the Christopher Award and L.L. Winship/PEN New England Award in 1990 (both for *House of Light*) and the National Book award in 1992 (for *New and Selected Poems*) and many more. Now some of you are saying, "OK, but I am not into poetry." Head into a bookstore or the store at the Province Lands Visitor Center and glance through one of her books. It may change your mind about poetry.

The Setting

Here is the interesting part. Much of her inspiration and communing with nature happened right here in the Cape Cod National Seashore on the Beech Forest Trail located in the Provincelands section of the park. When she wrote of ponds and water, she was referring to Blackwater Pond, the large pond at the end of the parking lot and next to the Beech Forest Trailhead. You can even enjoy the pond and commune with nature sitting right at the end of the Beech Forest Trail parking lot.

Oliver liked to tell the story of a time she walked the Beech Forest trail, felt inspired, and could not find a pen or pencil to write down her thoughts. After that she said she hid pencils in trees along the way so this would not happen again. However, she always made sure she carried a well-worn, three-by-five-inch notebook in her pocket. She once said that she did not put her poetry down in any order. She said that when she felt inspired, she would simply open the little notebook to any page and start writing.

Blackwater Pond

Now remember if you find a pencil hidden in a tree as you walk along Beech Forest Trail, it could be one of hers! However, if you are tempted to take it with you remember it is illegal to remove any object or artifact from federal property (including pens and pencils). If you want to leave a pencil as a tribute, don't. In that case you can be charged with littering.

To more fully share her experience with nature, take the loop around Beech Forest. The path around Blackwater Pond is about three-quarters of a mile. A loop extension past the end of the pond is another quarter mile. The extension loop has some steep log steps. Restrooms and a picnic area are near the parking area.

Additionally, Beech Forest is a great location for birding. Unfortunately, many birds are very friendly due to people improperly feeding them. Please don't feed them or any other wildlife, for that matter. Not only is it against the law, it is also dangerous for the animals to become too acclimated to humans. (This practice has led to aggressive animals and the park staff needing to kill them.)

Famous Locals

Just about everything is Provincetown has a history or story associated with it. Oliver's home at 535 Commercial Street is no exception. During the 1950s and 1960s, it was known as the Waterfront Apartments or by the occupants as "the Kibbutz" (because of many of the inhabitants who were Jewish). It was owned by Eldred Mowery, Jr., who was a classmate at Harvard of Robert F. Kennedy. Mowery was sent to jail for his part in an insurance scam concerning the theft of forty-one paintings from Hans Hoffman (The Father of Abstract Expressionism") who lived at 76 Commercial Street. Mowery was also a collaborator and friend of Norman Mailer, who also lived at the Waterfront (from 1961-62). Mailer and Mowery are buried near each other in Provincetown Cemetery #2 on Cemetery Road in Provincetown. Norman Mailer bought the brick house on the bay side at 627 Commercial Street in 1986. His estate sold it to Princess Tatiana von Furstenberg for $3.1 million in 2015.

And just in case you are interested, in 2022 a two bedroom, one bath, 698 square foot condo at 535 Commercial Street (the Waterfront Apartments) was estimated to be worth $1,341,538!

Al Jaffee's Parking Space Still Faintly Marked

Even parking spaces can have their own history here in Provincetown. (You could buy one in other parts of town in 2022 for between $50k and $80k, if you are interested.) If you look hard at the curbing at the first parking space at the Waterfront nearest to Fanizzi's Restaurant, you may still be able to make out the name Jaffee. The first space was the parking space of Al Jaffee, who was a Waterfront summer resident for many years. At one time next to the parking space, there was a sign that said that you couldn't park in the first space unless your name was Joyce. Joyce was Al Jaffee's wife, who died in January of 2021, just three months before Al turned a hundred. Al was a cartoonist for *Mad* magazine for many years starting in 1955. In 1964, he created the "fold-in" as *Mad's* answer to the *Playboy* magazine "fold-out." The fold-in allowed readers to change the images or text on a magazine page to a different image or text by folding the previous or following page partially over it. Al Jaffee died in early 2023 at the age of 102.

To Visit

Location: Beech Forest, Cape Cod National Seashore: 36 Race Point Road, Provincetown. From Route 6 Provincetown: at the east end traffic light go north (towards the Atlantic Ocean) on Race Point Road about a half a mile. The Beech Forest parking lot is on the left.

Waterfront Apartments: 535 Commercial Street is just west of Fanizzi's Restaurant.

Norman Mailer's Home: The brick house on the left at 627 Commercial Street.

Norman Mailer's Grave: Provincetown Cemetery #2, Section "Alden A." From Route 6, head towards the bay and take your first right onto Cemetery Road. At the end of Cemetery Road, take a right onto Alden Street. Take the third entrance on the right into the cemetery, drive to the end of the road, and take a right. His grave is eight rows in on your right: A63, A64, and A65.

21. PROVINCETOWN: THE GHOST OF OLD HARBOR LIFE-SAVING STATION

Historic Sites

Ghosts and Ghouls and Mysterious Shapes

Overview

This is actually a story about a ghost who left one building after it was destroyed and took up residence in a second one that was moved to the same area several decades later. It is a new story that few will have heard: the Wandering Ghost from Peaked Hill Bars. It is also a tribute to the heroic (some may say crazy) surfmen of the United States Life-Saving Service.

The Station

We talked previously about the history of the Life-Saving Service and Life-Saving stations on Cape Cod. Only three of these stations remain. One is a private home; one is the Beachcomber Restaurant in Wellfleet; and the third is the Old Harbor Life-Saving Station and Museum in Provincetown. Old harbor was moved to its present location at Race Point Beach in 1977/78 from Chatham.

Old Harbor Life-Saving Station Museum

The Lyle Gun

For ten months a year, each station was manned by six to eight men, while the Keeper, who was in charge of the station, worked year-round. Life-saving men patrolled between the stations 24/7 through sun and storms looking for signs of people and ships in distress. If sailors and ships' passengers were in need of rescue, the life-savers would attempt to row a large boat out to the people in order to get them safely to shore. If the weather was too bad or the sea was too rough for the boat, a Lyle gun was hauled to the scene on a specially-built cart to aid in the rescue.

The Lyle gun was a small cannon that was used to shot a line to the ship so the sailors on board could pull heavier lines and a block and pulley system onto the ship. The Lyle gun could shoot a projectile about seven hundred yards, but with a storm swirling around it was very difficult to use at that distance. Even though the Life-Saving Service was deactivated in the early 1940s, and in 1952 the Coast Guard substituted rockets for Lyle gun projectiles to send lines to ships, a Lyle gun was pulled out of a museum and used to rescue fishermen from a "dragger" (a fishing boat that uses a drag net or trawl net to catch fish) off Herring Cove Beach near Provincetown just east of Race Point in 1962!

Once the block and pulley system was secured onto the ship, a 'breeches buoy' was pulled out to the ship. A breeches buoy is a life-saving ring with a pair of legless canvas pants sewn in. Stranded sailors would climb into the breeches buoy and be pulled back to the shore from the ship.

Several breeches buoys are currently available for view. An original one is located at the Truro Historical Museum at 6 Highland Light Road in North Truro, and the National Seashore has three others on display at the Old Harbor Life-Saving Station Museum, the Province Lands Visitor Center, and the Salt Pond Visitor Center in Eastham.

A Day in the Life of a Life-Saving Station

Life at a Life-Saving Station was not easy. There was a regular schedule of drills six days a week, isolation from friends and family because of location, and of course the walks along the beach no matter how bad the weather. They did have good food, though, and the men ate hardily. Each week one of the men at the Life-Saving Station was assigned to cook for the others. The man whose turn it was to cook could have his wife live at the station with him for his assigned week to "assist" in the cooking.

Unfortunately, sometimes even with all this continuous training things just did not go as planned when put to the test. This takes us to our tale. At 10:30 pm on February 12, 1894, men from the Peaked Hill Bars Station, two and a half miles southeast of Race Point, were called to action by one of the men assigned to patrol the area between this and the Race Point Life-Saving Station. The sleeping men were desperately needed by marooned sailors on board the wooden hulled ship *Charlie Ricardo*, which was coming from Calcutta with a load of tin and sugar. It had gone aground on a sandbar far from shore. Eric Lohman, the young cook for the week, was obligated to leave his tearful, pregnant wife Mary (his guest for his assigned cooking week) as duty called him into action. As the storm raged around the station, Mary climbed up to the watchtower on top of the station to keep a lookout for Eric and await his safe return.

Where is Eric?

When the life-savers arrived at the location, they realized that the swirling storm made it impossible to launch their life-saving boat. The Lyle gun had to be used. Due to blinding wind filled with snow, sleet, and sand, young Eric stood too close to the line attached to the Lyle gun projectile. When the cannon was fired, the line caught Eric around the ankle and carried him out to sea. Mary could hear the cannon firing from her perch in the watch tower, not realizing the tragedy that was unfolding.

Because the storm was so strong and the *Charlie Ricardo* had a wooden hull, it broke apart during the attempted rescue, and there were no survivors. The men from Peaked Hill Bar searched in vain for survivors and for Eric, but no trace of any of them could be found.

When the men and equipment finally returned to the station, Mary did not see Eric. Isaac C. Fisher, the Keeper at the time, climbed up to the tower and broke the news to Mary that her husband was lost at sea and probably would not be returning. Mary asked the Keeper to let her be alone in the tower to think and grieve for a few minutes. Several minutes later, a scream was heard. Distraught, Mary had jumped from the station's watchtower. Both she and the unborn baby she was carrying died on impact with the rock-hard, icy snow.

From that day forward, there have been stories of men on duty in the Peaked Hill Bar tower hearing faint crying and of people around the life-saving station actually seeing a ghost-like manifestation, perhaps of Mary Lohman in the tower late at night. It is said that sometimes a faint voice could be heard crying out, "Eric, Eric, come home!"

Peaked Hill Bars Life-Saving Station January 10, 1931 (Public Domain)

As an interesting (or creepy) aside, playwright Eugene O'Neill, who struggled with depression and alcoholism much of his life, moved into the then-abandoned Peaked Hill Bars Life-Saving Station (the name was changed from Bar to Bars in 1888) with his second wife Agnes Boulton in May of 1919. O'Neill's father had bought it for them as a wedding present. O'Neill is said to have penned *The Hairy Ape, S.S. Glencairn*, and a first draft of *Anna Christie* while there. He once told a friend that on some nights when he was drinking and lonely, a young woman named Mary would come by to keep him company. He thought that she might have been a "very strange" neighbor. The Peaked Hill Bars Station slid into the sea on January 10, 1931.

Mary's New Home

We know nothing of Mary's whereabouts from 1931 until the fall of 1978, which is when the Old Harbor Life-Saving Station was moved from Chatham to its current location just east of Race Point Beach.

It seems that Mary has now found a home in this nearest Life-Saving Station to the old Peaked Hill Bars Station. Several people swear that they have seen lights and a woman's figure in the Old Harbor tower, and others have even thought that they heard muffled crying while fishing near Old Harbor late at night. In the early 2000s, a couple from Albany, New York, said that as they were walking on the path to Old Harbor, a young girl in a nightgown-like outfit asked them if they had seen "Eric" and then turned and ran towards the life-saving station. Several other people have told similar stories about a distraught young girl coming to them as they enjoyed fires on the nearby beach.

Life Saving Drill Reenactment at the Old Harbor Life-Saving Station Museum

The Old Harbor Life-Saving Museum is a great place to visit. It is filled with history and artifacts of interest to both the young and old. On Thursday evenings during the summer, they even have a Life-Saving demonstration complete with the firing of the Lyle gun and the "rescue" of a marooned sailor down a line from the top of a "ship's mast" to the beach in a breeches buoy.

To Visit

Location: Old Harbor Life-Saving Station Museum. Route 6 to Provincetown. At the east end traffic light—the first one you will come to—turn right onto Race Point Road. Follow Race Point Road 2.3 miles to the Race Point Beach parking lot at the end of the road. Park near the right end of the lot nearest to the bath houses. Walk between the bath houses and the path to the beach for about fifty feet to the boardwalk leading to Old Harbor Life-Saving Station on the right. The Old Harbor Life-Saving Station Museum is open Friday through Monday from 2 to 4 pm. It is worth the trip. They even have a very special National Parks Passport stamp! Old Harbor has a free life-saving reenactment (including the firing of a Lyle gun and a breeches buoy rescue) on Thursday evenings at 5 pm during the summer.

Truro Historical Museum: Take Route 6 to Highland Road. Highland Road is marked by a big sign that says "Highland Light–Cape Cod Light." Follow the road east (towards the ocean). At the "T" at the end of the road take a right. After about 1,000 yards, turn left onto Highland Light Road. Parking lot is on the right, Highland House Museum is on your left, and Cape Cod Light is straight ahead.

*The Peaked Hill Bars Life-Saving Station was originally named Peaked Hill Bar Life-Saving Station (1873-1887) and later renamed Peaked Hill Bars Life-Saving Station (1888-1937) because of the numerous sandbars at Peaked Hill. The Atlantic off the Peaked Hill Bars Station is said to be one of the most dangerous areas on the United States coastline.

22. PROVINCETOWN: THE SMALLPOX CEMETERY AND PEST HOUSE

Historic Sites

Overview

One of the loneliest places in Provincetown is the smallpox cemetery. Even though it is a less-than-fifteen-minute walk from a major highway, five minutes from a favorite walking path, and is not very difficult to get to, no one tends to it, no one cleans it up, no relatives come to visit, and no one plants flowers or even stops by to spend a few minutes contemplating the poor souls resting there. Just fourteen small stones, a few just eighteen inches high, and a few broken stumps are just stuck between a hill and a bog. There is no signage or crosses. The stones of these poor souls who inhabit the cemetery are identified only by a number...no carvings, no names, no dates...just a number... some have been forgotten in the wet, cold ground for almost two-hundred-seventy-five years. Alone, shunned in death and forgotten...

Number 10 – Frank Sofrine (aka Small)
Died December 24, 1872

Smallpox

Smallpox was one of the deadliest diseases known to humans. No one knows how long it has been with us. Sanskrit medical writings from 1500 BCE describe a smallpox-like illness, and the mummy of Egyptian pharaoh Ramses V who died in 1157 BCE had similar pox scarring on his remains.

The disease was spread by close contact with respiratory droplets and from sores of infected persons along with infected bedding and clothing. About one in three of those infected died, usually during the second week of infection. Symptoms typically started with lethargy and a fever, and many times included sore throat, vomiting, and headache. A raised rash developed, and sores appeared inside the nose, mouth, and throat. Fluid-filled pustules spread over the body, and scabs formed and sloughed off. Most survivors had permanent scarring, and many times nose, lip, and ear tissue were lost. Corneal scarring and blindness also occurred. During the twentieth century, an estimated three hundred million people succumbed to it! The last known case was that of hospital worker, Ali Maow Maalin in Somalia in 1977. (In 2013 he finally died from a different disease: malaria at the age of fifty-nine.) Smallpox is the only human disease that has been eradicated by vaccination.

A line of Lonely Graves at the Smallpox Cemetery

Provincetown Disease

Legend has it that one of the first cases, if not the earliest known case of smallpox, in Provincetown was that of Thomas Ridley. He was buried alone deep in the woods behind what is now Montano's Restaurant on Route 6 in North Truro. It is in the middle of a deep forest. Few people (including me) have searched for it and actually found his grave.

Around 1848, during a smallpox outbreak in Provincetown, a small building was constructed in the woods far away from town to house those few smallpox victims. This was the pestilence house or "Pest House." The victims were buried a few hundred feet away. The Pest House and cemetery are located a few hundred yards north of present-day Route 6 near the intersection of Shank Painter Road. The victims were shunned, and the conditions in the Pest house were deplorable. While they had the services of a doctor, the house was a small, cold room where victims were sent to get better or die.

As the victims died, they were buried nearby with just a numbered stone as a marker. This was probably done to keep the victim's identity secret to spare the victim's families any problems they might have encountered from the locals. Victim fourteen died between 1855 and 1873, and the Pest House was removed shortly thereafter. All that remains of it is a large depression south of the grave markers about thirty yards down an indistinct path. As the past and memories faded, the cemetery was forgotten, and weeds and the ravages of time took over.

Most of the headstones have been damaged, leaving only four that are in relatively good condition: Numbers 5, 6, 9, and 10. In 1980, Lurana Higgins Cook, Hugh Francis Cook, Anne Gleason

MacIntyre, and John Stuart MacIntyre researched and wrote a book called *Provincetown Massachusetts Cemetery Inscriptions*.

Thanks to their research we believe we know the names that go with the numbers:

1. Adam Dyer – 5/9/1855 (age 22)
2. John Roberts – 5/15/1855
3. Monson W. Barnard – 5/19/1855
4. Elizabeth Hill – 5/20/1860 (age 51)
5. Kennis Ferguson – 5/20/1864 (age 22)
6. Antone Domingo – 11/1/1972 (widower, age 22, born in the Azores)
7. Mary Rogers – 11/8/1872 (age 25) (arrived from Boston on a boat on 11/2 and was immediately taken to the Pest House)
8. George G. Hallet – 11/26/1872 (age 31)
9. Tamsin Manuel – 11/27/1872 (died one month after her 73rd birthday)
10. Frank Sofrine (aka Small) – 12/24/1872
11. Manuel Terceira 12/24/1872
12. William H. Butler – 1/7/1873
13. John A. McDonald – 1/8/1873 (from Scotland)
14. Thomas Bussell – 5/28/1873 (arrived in Provincetown on 5/17)

May they rest in peace. In April of 2015, a memorial honoring the victims was placed near the entrance to the Winthrop Cemetery at the intersection of Winthrop and Court Streets.

To Visit

Location: Built at the bottom of a steep ravine on the lowlands northwest of Duck Pond. (Warning: Poison ivy and ticks are rampant in this area.) The trailhead is by the first parking area after Shank Painter Road (on the north side of Route 6). There is a sign by the road that tells you to "SCOOP YOUR DOG POOP." Follow the trail to a fire road sign chained across the path. You can either take the trail up the very steep hill to your right or go past this chain about thirty feet to a small area where the trail branches into three directions. Take the trail on the right that goes up the same hill and along the ridge. It is not for the faint of heart. You will eventually come to the end of the trail. It is a very steep drop down into the cemetery. I walked down this hill on the side of the trail; I wore tick-proof clothing and held onto bushes on the way down. The cemetery is surrounded by the hill on two of its three sides and wetlands on its third side. There are no makings or signs, just seven headstones (whole or in pieces). Don't forget to view the depression down the path to the right where the Pest House was located. I am sure that you will notice the granite post with 1803 and some words carved into it just before the chain marking the fire road. This is an old boundary marker that marked the location where you would be leaving Provincetown land and entering State of Massachusetts land. Of course, it is now where you are leaving Provincetown land and entering Cape Cod National Seashore land.

1803 Boundary Marker

23. PROVINCETOWN: THOSE LITTLE BLUE TILES MEMORIALIZING A TOWN THAT WAS

Historic Sites

Overview

Take your arm, hold it horizontally straight out from your shoulder, bend your elbow so your forearm is pointing straight up, and finally bend your fingers down so the tips are pointing to your wrist. If this were a model of Cape Cod, your fingernails would be named "Long Point."

For thousands of years, this whole area was settled by the Nauset tribe. On May 15 (O.S. May 5), 1602, a European, Bartholomew Gosnold, mapped the area and named the area "Shoal Hope." A few days later, after marveling at his catch of codfish, he renamed the area now known as Provincetown as "Cape Cod."

Province Lands

The Pilgrims arrived in the harbor on November 21 (O.S. November 11), 1620. They left six weeks later and settled in the

Plymouth area. (I wonder how many of the Pilgrims' descendants wish that they had bought just one acre of land in downtown Provincetown?)

In 1654, the governor of Plymouth Colony purchased the land we call Provincetown for the use of the Plymouth Colony for twelve axes, twelve hoes, twelve knives, six coats, two brass kettles and a box. A new Royal Charter was granted in 1692 that combined Massachusetts Bay Colony and Plymouth colony into the Province of Massachusetts Bay, and Cape Cod was renamed "Province Lands." So now you know why the National Seashore Visitor Center near Provincetown is named the "Province Lands Visitor Center!"

Marker on the Homes Floated from Long Point

In 1714, Truro annexed Province Lands, and the area was renamed the Precinct of Cape Cod, and in 1727 the Precinct of Cape Cod was incorporated as a township. The name the townspeople preferred was "Herringtown," but the Massachusetts General Court chose to name the area "Provincetown." Interestingly, the act of incorporation stated that the inhabitants of Provincetown could be "landholders" and not "landowners." The people of Provincetown received a "Quit Claim" as opposed to a "Warranty Deed" to their property, not an actual title (which the Province retained). When I bought my land in Truro in the 1960s, I received a Quit Claim Deed. I guess that I really don't own anything there. I wonder why I have to pay taxes on something I don't own…

Long Point

Now, let's return to Long Point. This is the fingertips part of our bent arm. In 1818, the first house was built there by John Atwood. If you study more history of Long Point, you will find that many of the home owners were Atwoods. Additional houses were built in the next several years until about thirty-eight houses were constructed. The isolated location was chosen for the remarkable fishing right off the beach and the easy production of salt, a valuable commodity at the time. Long Point Light was built in 1827 to warn sailors away from the sandbars, some up to a quarter mile, that extended from Long Point out into Cape Cod Bay which are caused by the constant erosion that happens to this day along the Atlantic side of the Cape. Due in part to this erosion, a new lighthouse had to be built in 1875. The population of Long Point flourished, and in 1846, the town of Provincetown built a schoolhouse. At that time, there were thirty-eight families with sixty children and just under two hundred adults. Businesses were established including a bakery, general store, post office, several saltworks, and berthing for about twenty boats, used at that time primarily for cod fishing. All of this on the fingertips of your bent arm!

Unfortunately, this did not last long. Starting around 1850, the Long Point community began to decline. Transportation to and from Long Point was difficult, as inhabitants had to travel over four-and-a-half miles through the sand dunes to get to the mainland. There were economic factors, too. Salt production declined because open pit salt mining and later underground salt mining in upstate New York were much more economical and closer to major population areas; a larger harbor was needed to accommodate the rapidly growing fishing fleet and there was no fresh water available.

During the Civil War (1861-1865), fearing a blockade of the harbor, the federal government built a five-gun coastal artillery emplacement near the tip and a three-gun emplacement about two thousand feet to the southwest, along with barracks that housed ninety-eight soldiers on Long Point. One of the remaining homes became the officer's headquarters. The Long Point Batteries were known as "Fort Ridiculous" and "Fort Useless" by the locals because there did not seem to be any real purpose for having a military presence there, since they saw no service during the war.

Town-to-Go

Unlike most towns that are abandoned by their residents, the residents of Long Point literally took *all* of their possessions with them, including their houses! Some thirty of these houses were floated over the bay to Provincetown. It was said that the crossing was so smooth that the women cooked the meals for the men and served them when they landed on the beach! Most of these houses, known as "floaters," continue to exist in Provincetown. There are also a few in North Truro. How do you know which Provincetown houses were floaters? Just look for the square blue tile with the drawing of a house and waves on the front of the homes. Most of the homes are on Commercial Street in the West End, though there are a few on Bradford Street and in the East End near the Provincetown Art Association and Museum (PAAM) also on Commercial Street. The barracks that housed soldiers at Forts Ridiculous and Useless now resides at 473 Commercial Street.

The building at 256 Bradford Street, the former Long Point Post Office built there circa 1830, was also a floater. Other floaters now located on Bradford include number 200, built circa 1850 and originally a stable, and 301, built circa 1820 and owned by Eldridge Smith, another one of the founders of Long Point. I have listed a website below that has more information.

Only a few remnants of the Long Point community remain. Two mounds of sand are the only remaining evidence of the Long Point Batteries from the Civil War period. By the water, two rows of pilings from a wharf and the skeleton of a hull of a brig on the beach are all that remain of the Cape Cod Oil Works. There is also the lighthouse, constructed in 1875 and operated by solar power since 1981, and remains of an oil house constructed in 1904. A nearby mound of sand is topped by a wooden cross as a memorial to Charles Darby, a Provincetown soldier, who was killed in action during World War ll.

To Visit

Location: To see the "floaters," look for the blue tiles on two houses just before you pass PAAM when driving down Commercial Street. On the West End, there are many more "floaters" near "Dog Beach."

If you really want to visit Long Point, it's about a two-and-a-quarter-mile walk starting at the Provincetown jetty (West End Dike) at the end of Route 6. (Note that this route can be dangerous. It is not uncommon for people to slip or trip on the jetty or get stranded on Long Point if the tide is high.) In the summer, you can skip all of that bother by simply hopping a boat that takes people between Macmillan Pier and Long Point! It is a neat beach trip on a nice summer day. Don't forget sunscreen and anything else you might need.

For a wonderful description and history of many of the floaters see: *Provincetown: The History of Provincetown Told Through its Built Environment* at https://buildingprovincetown.wordpress.com/category/long-point-floaters/

24. PROVINCETOWN: THE OLDEST HOUSE IN PROVINCETOWN

Historic Sites

Overview

It is always fun to look for superlatives: the largest, smallest, first, thinnest, best, friendliest, highest, oldest, etc. Perhaps we just like to see the beginning or end of things. It makes life a tight little package. Unfortunately, superlatives are not always easy to come by, and when found, it can be difficult to locate the definitive example. Our search for the "oldest house" in Provincetown was just such a quest.

Current Oldest House

At the present time, the "honor" goes to the house at 72 Commercial Street in the town's West End. It really is very old and a beautiful example of a typical Cape Cod style house.

We do know a bit of the house's history. We know that it was built by a ship's carpenter by the name of Seth Nickerson (1733-1789). It is estimated that the house was built between 1746 to 1750. It is a great example of a full Cape Cod style home with two windows on each side of the front door and the chimney in the middle of the house. These types of homes are also referred to as a "Double Cape" due to the double windows on each side of the door. Most of the wood and the beams were salvaged from shipwrecks in and around the tip of Cape Cod, unfortunately a common practice at the time. Because of their source, many of the thick oak beams in the house are eight-by-eight inches thick!

Back in those days, many homes were designed and built to "ride out" high winds, blinding rain, and the sand shifting beneath them, just as ships had to ride out wind, waves, and storms on the ocean. As a result, the homes were often called "land craft." The chimney in this house is massive. It has to be, since three fireplaces are attached to it. It was constructed with a heavy wooden structure beneath it to support its estimated sixteen-ton weight. Incidentally, in 1755, five years after the house was thought to have been built, there were just ten homes and several outbuildings in Provincetown.

72 Commercial Street

In the old days, the house was sometimes actually called the "Seth Nickerson House," and the neighborhood was known as the "Nickerson" neighborhood because so many Nickersons lived in the area at the time. An article from 1949 indicates that it was Provincetown's first Baptist meeting house. The house remained in the Nickerson family until 1848 when Joshua Nickerson sold it to Joshua Paine for $750. It has changed hands at least 4 more times since.

Open and Closed

In 1927, F. Coulton and Elizabeth (Jenkinson) Waugh, two well-known artists of the time, bought the house and opened it to the public. They made the room to the right of the door into a Ship Model Shop, and the room on the left became the Hooked Rug Shop. The Waughs owned so many properties in the area that the neighborhood became known as "Waughville."

John and Adelaide Gregory owned the house from 1944 to 1995. John was a photographer, printer, and painter and Adelaide, a concert pianist. Here Adelaide gave piano lessons and public concerts, and both gave public tours of the house while John played music from his large 78 R.P.M. collection. (OK young'uns: 78 R.P.M. stands for seventy-eight Revolutions Per Minute. In olden times, records (those flat black discs old people bought recorded music on) were made to be played at certain speeds: 78, 45, 33, etc. The slower the speed, the more could be recorded on a disc.) In the 1950s, the Gregorys opened the "Ship-Shape Tea Room" in the house, where they served coffee, tea, pastries, and sandwiches.

The house changed hands in 1996 for $375,000 and again in November of 2018 for $880,000. In 2021, it was assessed at $1.7 million. I am sure that it is worth at least double that now.

The owners closed the house to the public and wish to remain undisturbed in their retreat. Please don't bother them or ask to see the exterior or interior of their home or gawk at the house.

Fun Facts

Here are some other interesting tidbits about a few old buildings in Provincetown: in 1795, the townspeople actually voted *not* to allow a Methodist Church to be built in town. In 1798, the Pease's Tavern was built, later becoming the Union House and, finally, the Atlantic House. Provincetown's oldest hotel, The Pilgrim House, was first opened in 1810. The Red Inn near the West End rotary was built in 1850.

To Visit

Location: 72 Commercial Street, Provincetown. Drive down Commercial Street until you see an octagonal-shaped house on the right-hand side of the street, followed by Soper Street and finally number 72 Commercial St. Please do not disturb the occupants or the surrounding neighborhood. There are many beautiful interior photographs of the house online.

25. PROVINCETOWN: THE REAL PLYMOUTH (ROCK) SAND

History Sites

Overview

I can remember in history class that I learned about the Pilgrims arriving in America. It went something like this: In 1620, they set sail aboard the *Mayflower* from Plymouth, England, in search of religious freedom. After a harrowing sixty-six-day voyage, they landed in Plymouth, Massachusetts. A group of them took a small boat to shore and stepped onto Plymouth Rock, at which point they were very grateful and probably shouted somethings like, "Hip Hip Hooray! Hip Hip Hooray! Hip Hip Hooray! We have finally landed in Vespucciland!"

The Real Deal

While we know that really was not what happened in 1620, it is pretty close to what I was taught. Here is the real, abbreviated story:

The Pilgrims set sail from Plymouth, England, on September 16 (O.S. September 6), 1620. After a horrendous sixty-six-day ocean voyage they sighted land on November 19 (O.S. November

9), 1620. The wind and waves were so bad and the weather so harsh that they waited until November 21 (O.S. November 11) to finally drop anchor.

William Bradford wrote about the landing:

> *Being thus arived in good harboring brought safe to land, they fell upon their knees & blessed y'e God in heaven who brought them over y'e vast & furious ocean, and delivered them from all y'e periles & miseries therof, againe to set their feete on y'e firme and stable earth, their proper elemente.* (1)

The Pilgrims finally set foot on "Cap-codd" or" Cap-Cod" in the new world, NOT in Plymouth but right here where Provincetown is today. A map of the location can be found in the book *Mourt's Relation: A Journal of the Pilgrims at Plymouth* written by Edward Winslow and published in 1622. Just to clarify a few terms: of the one-hundred-two passengers on the Mayflower, only forty-one were Puritan separatists. Sixty-one were not Puritans and were known at the time as "Strangers." There was also a crew of thirty-seven. At the time, and really well into the 1800s, Puritans were not called "Puritans" but rather "Brownists" after Robert Browne, an English religious reformer. They were later called "Pilgrims." At first their movement from England to North America was called the "Brownist Emigration."

Finding the Cape rather inhospitable, with poor soil for farming, dreary weather, and poor hunting, the Pilgrims and Strangers left Provincetown and sailed south and west to the abandoned Wampanoag village of Patuxet. Here they landed on December 16 (O.S. December 6*), 1620, in what is now modern-day Plymouth Harbor. Over the course of time, this location has had numerous names, originating with the Wampanoag name "Patuxet" to finally being renamed "Plymouth." It was here....

the Pilgrim Fathers first set foot December, 1620 upon bare rock on the bleak coast of Massachusetts Bay, while all around the earth was covered with deep snow... (2).

A disease (some say smallpox or a plague but more recently thought to be leptospirosis) had wiped out the population of Native Americans at Patuxet three years earlier. The disease had spread around the village so quickly that the Pilgrims found hundreds of unburied skeletons in the dwellings.

The reasons I bring all this up is: (1) The Pilgrims arrived in Provincetown first and not Plymouth, (2) a little history is good for you, and (3) you can get an idea of the approximate location of the first landing by going all the way to the little traffic circle at the end of Route 6 and walking back down Commercial Street to the Red Inn. Somewhere around the Inn is thought to be the site of the first landing. The West End rotary surrounds a little park, and in this park you will find a small monument commemorating the landing of the Pilgrims near this location.

Monument Commemorating the Landing of the Pilgrims in Provincetown Harbor

On September 17, 2020, the United States Postal Service issued a stamp commemorating the 400th anniversary of the landing of the Mayflower. It was a painting of the Mayflower...the script at the bottom of the stamp read: "Mayflower in Plymouth Harbor".

While you are there, enjoy the view and take a walk on the breakwater. Remember it is a mile and a quarter one way. Be careful, though, the rocks on the breakwater are uneven and can be very slippery. Most people call it the West End or Long Point Breakwater or Causeway, but it is really a dike. A *breakwater* is a structure built to protect the shore from being pounded by waves. A *dike* is a structure built to keep land from being flooded.

To Visit

Location: Follow Route 6 to the end or follow Commercial Street in Provincetown to the end or follow Bradford Street to the end and turn left onto Route 6. You know you have arrived at your destination when you come to a traffic circle. The monument is in the little park in the center of the circle. Walk up Commercial Street to the Red Inn. This is the approximate location where the Pilgrims came ashore.

(1) William Bradford's early account of Plymouth Colony. From 1898 printed edition. Online: https://virginia-anthology.org/william-bradford-of-plymouth-plantation/

(2) Losing, B.J. (1860). *A Pictorial History of the United States*, New York: Mason Bros.

Made in United States
North Haven, CT
05 June 2023